KETO MEAL]

Tasty Recipes + 28 Days Meal Plan to Eliminate Abdominal Fat, Hot Flashes, Join Pain and Low Libido| Regain your Self-Confidence and Feel Tireless and Beautiful Again

Table of Contents

CHAPTER 7.   DINNER 69

INTRODUCTION

The Keto diet is the perfect diet for those who are looking to lose weight. The diet is based on using fat as fuel instead of carbohydrates. It reduces your intake of simple carbs to less than 50 grams a day and relies solely on fats and proteins for energy.

This high fat intake causes your body to use stored fat for fuel. The result is weight loss without exercise. Once you reach your goal weight, you can start eating a more carbohydrate-based diet. You will lose that weight, but without the diet's negative effects such as fatigue or cravings.

This diet limits the amount of carbs you can eat in order to turn your body into a fat burning machine. You'll eat a lot more fat than you do now. Most people find that eating so much fat gives them more energy when they're working out at the gym or playing sports.

The keto diet is great for weight loss because it pushes you to consume more fats and less carbs. But if you think that's all the good the keto diet has to offer, think again! The keto diet also offers many other benefits including a greater sensitivity to insulin and better cholesterol levels. Plus, it can even improve your memory!

It is one of the most popular diets going today. It's easy to follow, offers many benefits, and is highly effective at improving your health when you do it correctly.

Keto diet side effects can be caused by many factors such as dehydration, electrolyte imbalances and certain medications. While there are many people that experience no side effects from it, others are known to experience such things as:

Tiredness or fatigue More muscle mass than normal Vomiting Headaches Irritability Constipation Muscle aches Feeling "blah" or down Heart palpitations Dizziness Decreased sex drive Irregular breathing Loss of appetite Blood sugar imbalance Muscle cramps Stomach pain Nausea Diarrhea Abdominal discomfort Herpes flaring up Eczema Rashes from skin allergies Sweating too much Bags in under eyes Dry eyes Drowsiness Decreased mental sharpness Epilepsy Height loss Inability to get pregnant Hormonal changes Increased heart rate Unpleasant smell from breath Decreased sexual drive While no one knows for sure why this happens.. There are many theories about how it may work. One theory is that the ketogenic diet may reduce the amount of insulin or increase the sensitivity of cells in the body that respond to excess glucose levels so they are better able to remove glucose before its toxic levels build up in your blood.

The ketogenic diet—or keto diet, for short—is increasingly popular in the United States as a weight-loss strategy. But how does it work? And do you need to go on it to lose weight? Keep reading to find out more about the keto diet and how it might benefit you.

The ketogenic diet is a dietary therapy that involves following a high-fat, low-carbohydrate approach. On the keto diet, you eat a lot of fat, a little protein, and only small amounts of carbs. The goal of the diet isn't to go into ketosis, or the state of ketosis itself—which occurs when your body uses fat stores as its primary source of fuel instead of carbohydrates (like bread). Instead, keto dieters simply want to push their bodies into the state of using fat as fuel instead of glucose (sugar).

CHAPTER 1.   KETO DIET BASICS

WHY IS GOOD THE KETO DIET

When you are on the keto diet, you want to make sure that you get all the nutrients that your body needs. The best way to do that is to eat foods that are rich in vitamins and minerals. Keto Meal Prep provides an easy way to make sure you are getting all of the nutrients you need.

Keto meal prep is a great way to keep your daily intake of protein and fats as low as possible while still having plenty of vegetables, fruits, and whole grains. Baked goods are a great way to save space and time when it comes to making sure you have all of the ingredients you need for your keto recipes.

This diet is very popular these days and for good reason. It can help you burn fat, lose weight, and feel better overall. However, not everyone needs the keto diet. If you want to lose weight and only use the keto diet sparingly as needed, there are a number of other healthy ways to go about it.

So what is keto? This diet is a low-carbohydrate, moderate-protein and high-fat diet designed to induce ketosis. To be more specific, it is a high-fat, medium-protein, and very low-carbohydrate diet. By eating this way you are able to enter a metabolic state called ketosis.

When you enter into ketosis your body switches from using glucose as its primary energy source to using fats as its primary energy source. Your body breaks down fat & converts it into fatty acids (structural molecules of fats). That's why the ketogenic diet is so effective at helping people lose weight and increase overall health because it helps them break down and use stored fat as their primary energy source instead of carbs that are converted into glucose (a type of sugar).

Your body uses up many carbohydrates when you eat them every day. They are converted into glucose in your digestive tract. Glucose is then transported through your bloodstream to every cell in your body where it provides energy for all of your cells. It also creates small waste products (called waste and carbon dioxide) that are eliminated through your lungs every time you breathe out.

WHAT IS KETO MEAL PREP

Keto meal prep is a way to incorporate more vegetables into your diet. Meal prep is a great way to add variety, and it allows you to eat healthy foods that you may not normally be able to eat because of time constraints or other eating restrictions. Meal prepping can help you lose weight, and if you don't have the time or energy to prepare healthy meals for yourself, meal prepping can make it easier to stick with your diet.

HOW KETO DIET WORKS

The keto diet is an extremely effective way to lose weight and keep it off. It's now becoming more popular and can be learned in as little as 2 days. Keto meal prepping is exactly what you need to do in order to keep your diet on track and lose weight.

Keto meal prepping isn't difficult at all, and it's the best way to go because it makes your prep and cleanup incredibly easy. The keto diet works by running your body into a state of ketosis. This is achieved by eating a low-carbohydrate, high-fat diet, which forces your body to burn fat rather than carbohydrates for fuel. This causes your body to begin burning fat for energy.

The way you eat will depend on your goals. Some people want to lose weight, others are looking for muscle gain and others just want to maintain their current weight. At Keto Meal Prep, we offer a complete line of high quality Keto products that will aid you in reaching your goals and provide you with a great meal plan so you can stay on track with your diet in both the short-term and long-term.

BENEFITS OF KETO DIET

When trying to follow a keto diet, there are a ton of benefits to staying in ketosis that you may not know about. Surprisingly, following the keto diet can be more advantageous than not following it at all! Ketosis is the natural state of metabolism for your body after fasting or when eating very low carb diets. It's when your body runs off of fats for fuel instead of carbohydrate and protein. It is also when your body enters into a state of satiety, meaning you won't be hungry for any calories as your body is using fat as its primary fuel source.

When you're on a keto diet, you can choose from many options and incorporate new recipes. The benefits to following a keto diet are endless. First, on this diet you consume very few carbohydrates and almost no protein or fat. This is because the goal of this diet is to force your body to burn fat instead of carbohydrates which can reduce hunger and control blood sugar levels. Want proof? Check out this article on the benefits to following a keto diet!

Keto meal plans are basically just meal plans that are designed around a specific macro or macronutrient ratio for fueling your body. On a typical ketogenic diet plan, proteins make up more than 90 percent of your diet, while fats take up only about 6 percent of your caloric intake. This means that you'll need to be eating an enormous amount of food even while following a low-carbohydrate diet such as the keto diet!

CHAPTER 2.   BENEFITS KETO OVER 50

LOSING WEIGHT

For most people, this is the foremost benefit of switching to keto! Their previous diet method may have stalled for them or they were noticing weight creeping back on. With keto, studies have shown that people have been able to follow this diet and relay fewer hunger pangs and suppressed appetite while losing weight at the same time! You are minimizing your carbohydrate intake, which means fewer blood sugar spikes. Often, those fluctuations in blood sugar levels make you feel more hungry and prone to snacking in between meals. Instead, by guiding the body towards ketosis, you are eating a more fulfilling diet of fat and protein and harnessing energy from ketone molecules instead of glucose. Studies show that low-carb diets are very effective in reducing visceral fat (the fat you commonly see around the abdomen that increases as you become obese). This reduces your risk of obesity and improves your health in the long run.

REDUCE THE RISK OF TYPE 2 DIABETES:

As we mentioned in the previous chapter, the problem with carbohydrates is how unstable they make blood sugar levels. This can be very dangerous for people who have diabetes or are pre-diabetic because of unstable blood sugar levels or family history. Keto is a great option because of the minimal intake of carbohydrates it requires. Instead, you are harnessing most of your calories from fat or protein which will not cause blood sugar spikes and ultimately less pressure on the pancreas to secrete insulin. Many studies have found that diabetes patients who followed the keto diet lost more weight and ultimately reduced their fasting glucose levels. This is monumental news for patients who have unstable blood sugar levels or are hoping to avoid or reduce their diabetes medication intake.

LOWER YOUR CHANCES OF HAVING HEART DISEASE:

Most people assume that following keto that is so high in fat content has to increase your risk of coronary heart disease or heart attack. But the research proves otherwise! Research shows that switching to keto can lower your blood pressure, increase your HDL good cholesterol, and reduce your triglyceride fatty acid levels. That's because the fats you are consuming on keto are healthy and high-quality fats so they reverse many unhealthy symptoms of heart disease. They boost your "good" HDL cholesterol numbers and decrease your "bad" LDL cholesterol numbers. It also decreases the level of triglyceride fatty acids in the bloodstream. A top-level of these can lead to stroke, heart attack, or premature death. And what are the top levels of fatty acids linked to?

DECREASES INFLAMMATION IN THE BODY

Inflammation on its own is a natural response by the body's immune system, but when it becomes uncontrollable, it can lead to an array of health problems; some severe, and some minor. The health concerns include acne, autoimmune conditions, arthritis, psoriasis, irritable bowel syndrome, and even acne and eczema. Often, removing sugars and carbohydrates from your diet can help patients of these diseases avoid flare-ups - and the delightful news is keto does just that! A 2008 research study found that keto decreased a blood marker linked to high inflammation in the body by nearly 40%. This is glorious news for people who may suffer from an inflammatory disease and want to change their diet to see improvement.

INCREASES YOUR MENTAL FUNCTIONING LEVEL

As we elaborated earlier, the energy-rich ketones can boost the body's physical and mental levels of alertness. Research has shown that keto is a much better energy source for the brain than simple sugar glucose molecules are. With nearly 75% of your diet coming from healthy fats, the brain's neural cells and mitochondria have a better source of energy to function at the highest level. Some studies have tested patients on the keto diet and found they had higher cognitive functioning, better memory recall, and were less susceptible to memory loss. The keto diet can even decrease the occurrence of migraines which can be very detrimental to patients.

DECREASES RISK OF DISEASES LIKE ALZHEIMER'S, PARKINSON'S, AND EPILEPSY.

They created the keto diet in the 1920s to combat epilepsy in children. From there, research has found that keto can improve your cognitive functioning level and protect brain cells from injury or damage. This is very good to reduce the risk of neurodegenerative disease which begins in the brain because of neural cells mutating and functioning with damaged parts or lower than peak optimal functioning. Studies have found that the following keto can improve the mental functioning of patients who suffer from diseases like Alzheimer's or Parkinson's. These neurodegenerative diseases sadly have no cure, but the keto diet could improve symptoms as they progress. Researchers believe that it's because of cutting out carbs from your diet, which reduces the occurrence of blood sugar spikes that the body's neural cells have to keep adjusting to.

PCOS (POLYCYSTIC OVARY SYNDROME)

Women who have PCOS suffer from infertility, which can be very heartbreaking for young couples trying to start a family. There is no cure for this condition, but we believe it's related to many similar diabetic symptoms like obesity and a high level of insulin. This causes the body to produce more sex hormones which can lead to infertility. The keto diet has become a popular method that tries to regulate insulin and hormone levels and could increase a woman's chances of getting pregnant.

LOWER LEVELS OF TRIGLYCERIDES

Many people do not know what triglycerides are. Triglycerides are molecules of fat in your blood. They are known to circulate the bloodstream and can be very dangerous. High levels of triglycerides can cause heart failures and heart diseases. However, Keto is known to reduce these levels.

REDUCES ACNE

Although acne is mostly suffered by those who are young, there are cases of people above 50 having it. Moreover, Keto is not only for persons after 50. Acne is not only caused by blocked pores. There are quite some things proven to cause it. One of these things is your blood sugar. When you consume processed and refined carbs, it affects gut bacteria and results in the fluctuation of blood sugar levels. When the gut bacteria and sugar levels are affected, the skin suffers. However, when you embark on the Keto diet, you cut off on carbs intake, which means that in the very first place, your gut bacteria will not be affected, thereby cutting off that avenue to develop.

INCREASES HDL LEVELS

HDL refers to high-density lipoprotein. When your HDL levels are compared to your LDL levels and are not found low, your risk of developing heart disease is lowered. This is great for persons over 50 as heart diseases suddenly become more probable. Eating fats and reducing your intake of carbohydrates is one of the most certain ways to increase your high-density lipoprotein levels.

REDUCES LDL LEVELS

High levels of LDL can be very problematic when you attain 50. This is because LDL refers to bad cholesterol. People with high levels of this cholesterol are more likely to get heart attacks. When you reduce the number of carbs you consume, you will increase the size of bad LDL particles. However, this will result in the reduction of the total LDL particles as they would have increased in size. Smaller LDL particles have been linked to heart diseases, while larger ones have been proven to have lower risks attached.

KETOGENIC DIET FOR POSTMENOPAUSAL WOMEN

The keto diet can be beneficial to women at the age of 50 and older who are going through menopause. There are three phases of menopause that all women go through, which are perimenopause, menopause, and postmenopause. You are considered postmenopausal when you have not had a period in over 12 months.

Most women go through menopause in their late 40s to early 50s, but not all women experience it at the same age as other women, and you might find that you have gone through menopause early or that you are yet to go through menopause.

When you start menopause will depend on various factors, such as when other women in your family like your mother, sister, or grandmother experienced menopause, whether you use oral contraceptives or not, your weight, how many pregnancies you have had, whether you smoke or drink alcohol, and whether you are physically active or not.

Perimenopause is the phase you go through before you become menopausal and usually begins when you are in your mid to late 40s. When you go through perimenopause, your body will go through new changes, and you will start to experience various symptoms such as hot flashes, being unable to sleep at night or being restless during the night, feeling lethargic, vaginal dryness, breaking into hot sweats in the night, not being able to remember things or struggling to focus, and having mood swings.

These symptoms are usually the worst in the perimenopause phase and continue on into the menopause and postmenopause stage. However, many women who do not experience these symptoms severely in the perimenopausal stage might find that these symptoms worsen in the later menopausal and postmenopausal phases. When a woman becomes perimenopausal, her estrogen and progesterone levels in her body decrease. Estrogen and progesterone are hormones that are used in a woman's body to help support the functioning of the reproductive system and to keep a woman's menstrual cycle regular. When these hormones decrease, your reproductive system will release fewer eggs, and your menstrual cycle will no longer be regular.

When you were younger, the estrogen hormone would work to distribute your stored fat into your hips and thighs. However, as you become older and your estrogen decreases, this fat is redirected to your stomach area. When fat stores in your stomach area, you become more at risk of developing heart disease, insulin resistance, and type 2 diabetes.

With the reduction of estrogen in the body and removing energy sources like sugar and carbohydrates from your diet, your body and brain will create ketones that will use the fat that you consume from the keto diet as an alternative source of energy. Your hot flashes stem from receiving glucose in your brain, and when your brain no longer receives glucose from your diet, the severity and frequency of hot flashes that you experience is reduced. The keto diet has also been found to improve your mood and protect your memory against remembering things and improve your concentration.

It is suggested that when you follow the keto diet and you are going through menopause that you should further restrict your carbohydrate intake from the allowed 50 grams per day to between 20 to 30 grams per day so that your body goes into ketosis and can successfully help to relieve these symptoms.

WHAT LIFESTYLE TO COMBINE WITH THE KETOGENIC DIET TO HAVE A HEALTHY

The Keto Diet and Intermittent Fasting

Of course, everyone should watch out for their nutrition and not overeat. This is undoubtedly good for health. Many of us periodically notice that after a dense meal we become lethargic, drowsiness appears, the ability to work decreases, and we don't want anything except to lie down. All this testifies to the fact that the less we eat, the more cheerful we feel. But do not go to extremes. 1-2 times a week is enough to arrange fasting days, reducing the usual amount of food consumed or filling the diet only with fruits and vegetables. If you still want to experience any of the Intermittent Fasting schemes, make sure that it does not harm you

COMBINING THE KETO DIET WITH INTERMITTENT FASTING

Combining the keto diet with intermittent fasting is the most natural thing to do as both the ideas complement each other perfectly and lead to faster fat-burning besides other health benefits.

The most important thing that you'd need to do is make changes in your macronutrient proportions and implement them in your diet plan.

The ideal macronutrient ratio should be:

- Fat: 70-75%
- Protein: 20-25%
- Carbs: 5-10%

Fat

You should include a lot of healthy fats in your diet.

Healthy fats such as nuts and seeds should make the cut.

You can also include fat-rich fruits like avocadoes.

Grass-fed meats and fatty fish are also good things to include in your diet.

You should exclude fast foods and deep-fried foods. Although they have a lot of fat, the fat is generally trans fats that should be avoided. These food items also have a lot of sugar and salt that you'd like to avoid as they can come in the way of ketosis and are very bad for your heart health and sugar levels.

Although the fat percentage is very high in a keto diet, it doesn't mean that you will have to eat a lot of fat. The fat is high in calories and hence eating even small quantities of fat would make up for the percentage.

Proteins

You can include grass-fed lean meat into your diet for completing the protein content.

Legumes also have a lot of protein, and you can include them in your daily diet. You can eat sprouts as they are a cleaner source of rich protein.

Tofu, cottage cheese, and dairy product, and egg whites also provide protein in good quantities.

Fish are also high in protein, and they also provide Omega-3 fatty acids that are good for your heart.

Carbs

You'll have to be careful while including carbs in your diet. You must only choose high-fiber sources of carbs in your diet. Complex carbs obtained from whole grains can make a part of the carb ratio.

Your focus should be to include as much non-starchy leafy greens into your diet as possible. This is the only type of carbs that you can consume without worrying about the number of calories you are ingesting. You should have at least 7-10 cups of non-starchy leafy green in your diet daily.

These vegetables will fill you up and make you feel satiated much faster. The soluble fiber in these vegetables makes a gel-like substance in your gut that cleans the gut and helps in easing insulin resistance too.

COMBINING THE KETOGENIC AND MEDITERRANEAN DIETS

First, they offer similar health benefits, making them compatible. Both lower cholesterol and focus on the nutrients found in fresh vegetables. They also both eliminate artificial foods, refined sugar, and additives. The main reason to hybridize them, however, is that the Mediterranean diet can make the ketogenic diet healthier.

The ketogenic diet is often criticized because it can lead to micronutrient deficiency. It can also become an unbalanced diet too full of red meat, dairy, and not enough vegetables. When you emphasise Mediterranean foods like olive oil and seafood, it can help restore balance and nutrients to your eating. To fill in the space left by reducing red meat and dairy, you can easily add more vegetables. More health benefits result.

The philosophy of the Mediterranean diet also impacts the ketogenic diet in a very positive way. When you're trying to get (and stay) in ketosis, you will be tempted to focus too much on numbers - the number of carbs you're eating, your ketone level, how many calories you're eating, and so on. The Mediterranean diet emphasizes enjoying the food you make, cooking and eating with loved ones, and being active.

Combining the ketogenic and Mediterranean diet can make the restrictiveness of the keto diet a bit easier and healthier, since you focus a lot on seafood, vegetables, olive oil, and non-diet habits like exercise and spending time with loved ones.

LIFE AND STAY FIT (EXERCISES)

Dieticians and physical health professionals recommend certain exercise practices for women going through Keto. This chapter puts all of these recommended exercises in one place so you won't have to look anywhere else.

Strength training helps women maintain muscle tone, as you would expect, but that isn't all it does. Strength training shines the most in how it can directly trigger autophagy. Overall, strength training exercises are one of the best things you can do for your body.

Exercise is very hard to get people to do at any age, but it is especially important for people over 50 to get into strength training. By this point in life, it isn't about getting abs or toned arms. It is about keeping your muscles engaged so you can continue to use them for practical purposes.

The statistics on muscle loss paint a clear picture. One study demonstrated that adults between 30 and 80 lose up to forty percent of their strength if they are sedentary.

Keeping your existing muscle mass doesn't mean you have to turn into some sort of superhero. It just means you can do normal things around the house, do your own shopping, take care of your lawn, and get up when you fall. Your muscle mass isn't all that matters here. Keeping up with strength training also maintains the density of your bones. Women over 50 need to be particularly cognizant of their bone density. When you have more fragile bones, you are at a much higher risk of injury when you fall down. When we are young, our bones are sturdy and elastic. We could repeatedly fall without any issues. But the older we get, the riskier it is to fall, because you may be at serious risk of injury.

Strength training will also help you burn fat. It won't do it as quickly as cardiovascular training, such as running on a treadmill, but it is better for you in other ways besides just losing weight.

Do 8-12 repetitions for every work out and give yourself a 30-60 second break in between reps. Take your time with each of them, and be sure to get in deep breaths throughout all of them. Don't take it too seriously: allow yourself to enjoy it and take it at your own pace. Do not stress about these

BEST EXERCISE ROUTINE

Walk 30 to 40 minutes every day.

Try to challenge yourself with short-term goals such as: "Only today I will do 45 minutes of exercise bikes" and then I will start the next day or two days later with another challenge. The same goes for food! This method is extremely effective in increasing motivation.

Limit the consumption of fat (which contributes to visceral fat) by avoiding potato chips, French fries, fast foods, industrial cakes and muffins and limiting ham and cheese.

Limit alcohol consumption as it is likely to end up as visceral fat.

No more added sugar! Try drinking your tea or coffee with no added sugar. Usually, it only takes a few days up to 2 weeks to get rid of this habit. Avoid sweet and soda drinks that contain tons of added sugar.

Replace the chocolate bars with oranges or apples. 1 bar of chocolate (250 kcal) contains 12 g of fat, 60 times more than what an apple (90 kcal) or an orange (60 kcal) contains!

Eat fruits and vegetables. For example: 1 orange or a banana for breakfast with a cup of green tea or thyme in boiling water.

Sleep at least 8 hours a night, as lack of sleep adversely affects mood and stimulates appetite and hunger.

Persevering! This is the key to success.

TIPS FOR LOSING WEIGHT OVER 50

Routines are essential on this diet, and it's something that will help you stay healthy as you age and become lost in your average weight. In this phase, we will be giving you tips and tricks to make this diet work better for you and help you get an idea of routines that you can put in place for yourself.

Learn How to Count Your Macros

This is especially important at the start of your journey. As time goes by, you will learn how to estimate your meals without using a food scale.

Prepare Your Kitchen for Your Keto-Friendly Food

Once you've made a choice, it's time to get rid of all the foods in your kitchen that aren't allowed in the keto diet. To do this, check the *Nutritional* labels of all the food items. Of course, there's no need to throw everything away. You can donate foods you don't need to food kitchens and other institutions that give food to the needy.

Purchase Some Keto Strips for Yourself

These are important so you can check your ketone levels and track your progress. You can purchase keto strips in pharmacies and online. For instance, some of the best keto strips available on Amazon are Perfect Keto Ketone Test Strips, Smackfat Ketone Strips, and One Earth Ketone Strips.

Find an Activity You Enjoy

When you have done enough exercise, you will know what activities you like. One way to encourage yourself to exercise more regularly is by making it entertaining than a chore. If possible, stick to your favorite activities, and you can get the most out of your exercises. Keep in mind that the activities you enjoy may not be effective or needed, so you need to find other exercises to compensate for, which you may not enjoy. For instance, if you like jogging, you can work your leg muscles, but your arms are not involved. So, you need to do pushups or other strength training exercises.

Check with a Healthcare Provider

Your dietitian can tell you whether a keto diet would work. Still, it helps to check in with your healthcare provider to ensure that you do not have any medical condition that prevents you from losing weight, such as hypothyroidism and polycystic ovary syndrome. It helps to know well in advance whether your body is even capable of losing fat in the first place before you commit and see no result, right?

Hydrate Properly

That means drinking enough water or herbal tea and ditch sweetened beverages or other drinks that contain sugar altogether. Making the transition will be difficult for the first few weeks, but your body will thank you for it. There is nothing healthier than good old plain water, and the recommended amount is 2 gallons a day.

Take Supplements

When you get older, your body starts to lose its ability to absorb certain nutrients, which leads to deficits. For example, vitamin B12 and folate are some of the most common nutrients that people over 50 lack. They have an impact on your mood, energy level, and weight loss rate.

Have the Right Mindset

Your mindset is one of the most important things you need to change when you've decided to follow the keto lifestyle. Without the right mindset, you might not stick with the diet long enough to enjoy all its benefits. Also, the proper mindset will keep you motivated to keep going no matter what challenges come your way.

Get Enough Sleep

Getting enough sleep helps your body regulate the hormones in your body. So try to aim for 7 to 9 hours of sleep a day. You can get more restful sleep by creating a nighttime routine that involves not looking at a computer, phone, or TV screen for at least 1 hour before bed. You can drink warm milk or water to help your body relax or even do 10 to 20 minutes of stretching to get a restful sleep.

Keep a Food Log

Then add the calories and divide by three to get an average. Now that you know how many takes, you can figure out how much you need to pay on average per day to reach your goals.

MACRO NUTRIENTS FOR ALL RECIPES

You have probably heard of macronutrients before, but what are they exactly? Macronutrients are an organic or chemical compound that is consumed to give us the nutritional value and energy we need in order to survive. The macronutrients include proteins, carbohydrates, and fats.

The keto diet requires you to keep your carbohydrate intake between 5% and 10% of your daily calories (Massod et al., 2020). This means you're allowed to eat anything from 0.70 to 1.7 ounces (20-50 gram) of carbs a day. Fat will make up the highest portion of your daily macros at between 55% to 60%, whereas protein will be 30% to 35%.

Fats

The first macro nutrient we will discuss is fats. As you already know, there are unsaturated and saturated fats. This nutrient is essential because Vitamins K, E, D, and A can only be consumed in this form. On the Ketogenic Diet, around 70% of your calories will be coming from fat.

Protein

Next, we have Protein. Protein can be composed of several different types of amino acids and are the "building blocks" of the human body. Interestingly enough. Nine out of the twenty amino acids cannot be made by the human body, which is why it needs to be supplemented into the diet.

While protein is essential for just about everyone, it is especially important for individuals who plan on staying physically active. Protein is responsible for building new muscle tissue and repairing other tissues. While there is a significant debate on how much protein people need, you can use the general rule of thumb to eat one gram of protein per pound of body weight.

Carbohydrates

On the Ketogenic Diet, you will not have to pay much attention to carbohydrates because they are going to make up such a small part of your diet. It should be noted that there are two general categories of carbohydrates: Complex and Simple.

Simple carbohydrates are sugar molecules that can be digested quickly for an energy boost while complex carbs come from whole-food plants and contain a higher amount of fiber, minerals, and vitamins. When you do eat carbs, these will be the ones that you will want to reach for.

If you wish to calculate the macros to reach your personal goals, I suggest using a calculator online to find your magic numbers. With that in mind, remember that it will be vital that you keep your carb count under 20g in a day.

HOW TO TRACK MACRONUTRIENTS

Although all the foods noted above are compatible with the keto diet, you need to know how much of each you should eat. You cannot munch on many of these foods to excess and expect to get great results. This is why you need to track your intake of your macronutrients. Tracking macronutrients is not just to ensure that you lose weight, but it is also a good tool to make sure that you do not starve yourself. You can make use of various online macronutrient calculators that can help you adjust your diet to your unique lifestyle. These calculators are important because the good ones calculate your level of activity as well. Nevertheless, the standard breakdown of daily macronutrient percentages is as follows:

- 5–10% carbs (30–50 g NET)

- 15–30% protein (0,6–1,0 g / lb)
- 70–80% fat

TIPS FOR AVOIDING KETO FLU

The anticipation of getting the keto flu can seem overwhelming, but the good news is that you are going to be able to help yourself. The reason people suffer from the keto flu for so long is that they have no idea what is happening to their body! Most people assume that they have to deal with the bad symptoms to get to the benefits of the diet. The truth is, these signs and symptoms from your body are like a cry for help! You don't just feel like junk for no reason! You will want to take the time to listen to your body and see how you can help yourself.

With that in mind, there are several steps you can take to help get you through the keto flu. Below, you will find some of my best tips to help you get over the keto flu and into ketosis with as little misery as possible.

Drink Up and Stay Hydrated

The number one tip I can give you as you begin the ketogenic diet is to stay hydrated! Even if you think that you are drinking enough water, you probably aren't. Staying hydrated should be your top priority as you begin the transition period into ketosis.

The best trick up my sleeve to help you drink more water through the day is to keep it in sight! I have a reusable water bottle that is by my side all day long. If you have a visual cue, it acts as an instant reminder to drink more water. I also suggest drinking a majority of the water during the day because it isn't so fun getting up to use the bathroom ten times a night.

Think Electrolytes

While we are on the topic of getting enough water, you will want to keep in mind that balancing your electrolytes is going to be just as important.

Before the ketogenic diet, many people don't have to worry about their electrolytes unless they are highly athletic. As mentioned earlier, your body is about to flush a mass majority of your water weight and electrolytes out of your system during this transition period. With that in mind, it should be noted that people lose electrolytes differently. The good news is that there are several ways for you to mitigate this imbalance.

Increase Fats

When your body begins switching over to its new source of energy, you are going to want to make sure that you are providing it with enough fat! Unfortunately, many people are shy about their fat intake when they are first starting their diet because we have been told our whole life that fat is bad! Now that your body is no longer using carbohydrates and sugar as energy, you will need to give your body what it needs!

As you increase your fat consumption while reducing your carb consumption, this will help push your body into using the fat as energy. If you need, you can always supplement with MCT oil to help increase your ketone levels. It is also a good idea to up your fat source and includes foods such as:

- Coconut Oil
- Cacao Butter
- Olive Oil
- Heavy Cream
- Ghee
- Grass-fed Butter
- Avocado Oil
- Bacon Fat
- Walnuts
- Chia Seeds
- Pecans
- Flaxseed
- Fatty Fish
- Sesame Seeds

Work it Out

The next way to help get you over the keto flu will be exercise! This can be hard for some people, especially if they are unable to work through the symptoms provided by the keto flu in the first place. For this reason, I highly suggest light exercise anywhere from two to three times a week.

As you begin moving your body, this will help the switch drastically. As soon as you get over the keto flu, you will be able to resume your normal exercise routine. If you are first starting out, I highly suggest low-intensity exercises. You can try something like yoga, swimming, or even a light walk. With exercise, you will be able to boost your metabolic flexibility and get over the keto flu before you even know it.

Exogenous Ketones

If none of the above work for you, you can always consider exogenous ketones. While your body is attempting to make the switch into ketosis, your body may not be producing enough ketones. For this reason, you may want to add ketone salts or exogenous ketones into your morning routine. By providing your body with what it needs, you can provide your system with ketones before you have even burned through the glycogen stores.

CHAPTER 3. FOODS TO EAT

SEAFOOD

Fishes and shellfishes are perfect for keto diets. Many fishes are rich in B vitamins, potassium, as well as selenium. Salmon, sardines, mackerel, and other fatty fish also pack a lot of omega-3 fats that help in regulating insulin levels. These are so low in carbs that it is negligible.

Shellfishes are a different story because some contain very few carbs whereas others pack plenty. Shrimps and most crabs are okay but beware of other types of shellfish.

VEGETABLES

Most vegetables pack a lot of nutrients that your body can greatly benefit from even though they are low in calories and carbs. Plus, some of them contain fiber, which helps with your bowel movement. Moreover, your body spends more energy breaking down and digesting food rich in fiber, so it helps with weight loss as well.

CHEESE

Milk, is not okay. You can get away with cheese though. Cheese is delicious and nutritious. Thankfully, although there are hundreds of types of cheese out there, all of them are low in carbs and full of fat. Eating cheese may even help your muscles and slow down aging.

AVOCADOS

Avocados are so famous nowadays in the health community that people associate the word "health" to avocados. This is for a very good reason because avocados are very healthy. They pack lots of vitamins and minerals such as potassium. Moreover, avocados are shown to help the body go into ketosis faster.

MEAT AND POULTRY

These two are the staple food in most keto diets. Most of the keto meals revolve around using these two ingredients. This is because they contain no carbs and pack plenty of vitamins and minerals. Moreover, they are a great source of protein.

EGGS

Eggs form the bulk of most food you will eat in a keto diet because they are the healthiest and most versatile food item of them all. Even a large egg contains so little carbs but packs plenty of protein, making it a perfect option for a keto diet.

Moreover, eggs are shown to have an appetite suppression effect, making you feel full for longer as well as regulating blood sugar levels. This leads to lower calorie intake for about a day. Just make sure to eat the entire egg because the nutrients are in the yolk.

COCONUT OIL

Coconut oil and other coconut-related products such as coconut milk and coconut powder are perfect for a keto diet. Coconut oil, especially, contain MCTs that are converted into ketones by the liver to be used as an immediate source of energy.

PLAIN GREEK YOGURT AND COTTAGE CHEESE

These two food items are rich in protein and a small number of carbs, small enough that you can safely include them into your keto diet. They also help suppress your appetite by making you feel full for longer and they can be eaten alone and are still delicious.

OLIVE OIL

Olive oil is very beneficial for your heart because it contains oleic acid that helps decrease heart disease risk factors. Extra-virgin olive oil is also rich in antioxidants. The best thing is that olive oil can be used as a main source of fat and it has no carbs. The same goes for olive.

NUTS AND SEEDS

These are also low in carbs but rich in fat. They are also healthy and have a lot of nutrients and fiber. They help reduce heart disease, cancer, depression, and other risks of diseases. The fiber in these also help make you feel full for longer, so you would consume fewer calories and your body would spend more calories digesting them.

BERRIES

Many fruits pack too many carbs that make them unsuitable in a keto diet, but not berries. They are low in carbs and high in fiber. Some of the best berries to include in your diet are blackberries, blueberries, raspberries, and strawberries.

BUTTER AND CREAM

These two food items pack plenty of fat and a very small amount of carbs, making them a good option to include in your keto diet.

SHIRATAKI NOODLES

If you love noodles and pasta but don't want to give up on them, then shirataki noodles are the perfect alternative. They are rich in water content and pack a lot of fiber, so that means low carbs and calories and hunger suppression.

UNSWEETENED COFFEE AND TEA

These two drinks are carb-free, so long as you don't add sugar, milk, or any other sweeteners. Both contain caffeine that improves your metabolism and suppresses your appetite. A word of warning to those who love light coffee and tea lattes, though. They are made with non-fat milk and contain a lot of carbs.

DARK CHOCOLATE AND COCOA POWDER

These two food items are delicious and contain antioxidants. Dark chocolate is associated with the reduction of heart disease risk by lowering the blood pressure. Just make sure that you choose only dark chocolate with at least 70% cocoa solids.

CHAPTER 4. FOODS TO AVOID

Because keto is a keto diet, that means you need to avoid high-carbs food. Some of the food you avoid is even healthy, but they just contain too many carbs. Here is a list of common food you should limit or avoid altogether.

BREAD AND GRAINS

Breads are a staple food in many countries. You have loaves, bagels, tortillas, the list goes on. However, no matter what form bread takes, they still pack a lot of carbs. The same applies to whole-grain as well because they are made from refined flour.

Depending on your daily carb limit, eating a sandwich or bagel can put you way over your daily limit. So if you really want to eat bread, it is best to make keto variants at home instead.

Grains such as rice, wheat, and oats pack a lot of carbs as well. So limit or avoid that as well.

FRUITS

Fruits are healthy for you. In fact, they have been linked to a lower risk of heart disease and cancer. However, there are a few that you need to avoid in your keto diets. The problem is that some of those foods pack quite a lot of carbs such as banana, raisins, dates, mango, and pear.

As a general rule, avoid sweet and dried fruits. Berries are an exception because they do not contain as much sugar and are rich in fiber. So you can still eat some of them, around 50 grams. Moderation is key.

VEGETABLES

Vegetables are just as healthy for your body. Most of the keto diet does not care how many vegetables you eat so long as they are low in starch. Vegetables that are rich in fiber can help with weight loss. For one, they make you feel full for longer so they help suppress your appetite. Another benefit is that your body would burn more calories to break and digest them. Moreover, they help control blood sugar and aid with your bowel movements.

But that also means you need to avoid or limit vegetables that are high in starch because they have more carbs than fiber. That includes corn, potato, sweet potato, and beets.

PASTA

Pasta is also a staple food in many countries. It is versatile and convenient. As with any other convenient food, pasta is rich in carbs. So when you are on your keto diet, spaghetti or any other types of pasta are not recommended. You can probably get away with it by eating a small portion, but that is not possible.

Thankfully, that does not mean you need to give up on it altogether. If you are craving pasta, you can try some other alternatives that are low in carbs such as spiralized veggies or shirataki noodles.

CEREAL

Cereal is also a huge offender because sugary breakfast cereals pack a lot of carbs. That also applies to "healthy cereals". Just because they use other words to describe their product does not mean that you should believe them. That also applies to oatmeal, whole-grain cereals, etc.

So when you eat a bowl of cereal when you are doing keto, you are already way over your carb limit, and we haven't even added milk into the equation! Therefore, avoid whole-grain cereal or cereals that we mention here altogether.

BEER

In reality, you can drink most alcoholic beverages in moderation without fear. For instance, dry wine does not have that many carbs and hard liquor has no carbs at all. So you can drink them without worry. Beer is an exception to this rule because it packs a lot of carbs.

Carbs in beers or other liquid are considered to be liquid carbs and they are even more dangerous than solid carbs. You see, when you eat food that is rich in carbs, you at least feel full. When you drink liquid carbs, you do not feel full as quickly so the appetite suppression effect is little.

SWEETENED YOGURT

Yogurt is actually very healthy because it is tasty and does not have that many carbs. It is a very versatile food to have in your keto diet. The problem comes when you consume yogurt variants that are rich in carbs such as fruit-flavored, low-fat, sweetened, or nonfat yogurt. A single serving of sweetened yogurt actually contains as many carbs as a single serving of dessert.

If you really love yogurt, you can get away with half a cup of plain Greek yogurt with 50 grams of raspberries or blackberries.

JUICE

Fruit juices are perhaps the worst beverage you can put into your system when you are on a keto diet. One may argue that juice provides some nutrients, but the problem is that it contains a lot of carbs that are very easy to digest. As a result, your blood sugar level will spike whenever you drink it. That also applies to vegetable juice because of the fast-digesting carbs present.

Another problem is that the brain does not process liquid carbs the same way as solid carbs. Solid carbs can help suppress appetite, but liquid carbs will only put your appetite into overdrive.

LOW-FAT AND FAT-FREE SALAD DRESSINGS

As mentioned previously, fruits and vegetables are largely okay so long as they are low in carbs. But if you have to buy salads, keep in mind that commercial dressings actually pack more carbs than you think, especially the fat-free and low-fat variants.

So if you want to enjoy your salad, dress your salad using creamy, full-fat dressing instead. To really cut down on carbs, you can use vinegar and olive oil, both of which are proven to help with heart health and aid in weight loss.

BEANS AND LEGUMES

These are also very nutritious as they are rich in fiber. Research has shown that eating these have many health benefits such as reduced inflammation and heart disease risk.

However, they are also rich in carbs. You may be able to enjoy a small amount of them when you are on your keto diet, but make sure you know exactly how much you can eat before you exceed your carb limit.

SUGAR

We mean sugar in any form, including honey. You may already be aware of what foods that contain lots of sugar such as cookies, candies, and cake are forbidden on a keto diet or any other form of diet that is designed to lose weight.

What you may not be aware of is that nature's sugar such as honey is just as rich in carbs as processed sugar. In fact, natural forms of sugar contain even more carbs.

Not only is that sugar, in general, rich in carbs, they also add little to no nutritional value to your meal. When you are on a keto diet, you need to keep in mind that your diet is going to consist of food that is rich in fiber and nutritious. So sugar is out of the question.

If you really want to sweeten your food you can just use a healthy sweetener instead because they do not add as many carbs to your food.

CHIPS AND CRACKERS

These two are some of the most popular snacks. What some people did not realize is that one packet of chips contain several servings and should not be all eaten in one go. The carbs can add up very quickly if you do not watch what you eat.

Crackers also pack a lot of carbs, although the amount varies based on how they are made. But even whole-wheat crackers contain a lot of carbs.

Due to how processed snacks are produced, it is difficult to stop yourself from eating everything within a short period of time. Therefore, it is advised that you avoid them altogether.

MILK

I mentioned previously that cereal contains a lot of carbs and a breakfast cereal will put you way over your carbs limit without you adding milk. Milk also contains a lot of carbs on its own. Therefore, avoid it if you can even though milk is a good source of many nutrients such as calcium, potassium, and other B vitamins.

Of course, that does not mean that you have to ditch milk altogether. You can get away with a tablespoon or two of milk for your coffee. But cream or half-and-half is better if you drink coffee frequently. These two contain very few carbs. But if you love to drink milk in large amounts or need it to make your favorite drinks, consider using coconut milk or unsweetened almond instead.

GLUTEN-FREE BAKED GOODS

Wheat, barley, and rye all contain gluten. Some people who have celiac disease still want to enjoy these delicacies but unable to because their gut will become inflamed in response to gluten. As such, gluten-free variants have been created to cater to their needs.

Gluten-free diets are very popular nowadays, but what many people don't seem to realize is that they pack quite a lot of carbs. That includes gluten-free bread, muffins, and other baked products. In reality, they contain even more carbs than their glutenous variant. Moreover, the flour used to make these gluten-free products are made from grains and starches. So when you consume a gluten-free bread, your blood sugar level spikes.

So, just stick to whole foods. Alternatively, you can use almond or coconut flour to make your own low-carb bread.

CHAPTER 5.   BREAKFAST

1.   EGGPLANT AND CHIVES SPREAD

Preparation Time: 5 minutes
Cooking Time: 20 minutes
Servings: 2
Ingredients:

- 3 eggplants
- Salt and black pepper to the taste
- 2 tbsp. chives, chopped
- 2 tbsp. olive oil
- 2 tsp. sweet paprika

Directions:
1.   Put the eggplants in your air fryer's basket and cook them for 20 minutes at 380°F.
2.   Peel the eggplants put them in a blender, add the rest of the ingredients, pulse well, divide into bowls and serve for breakfast.

Nutrition:
Calories: 190
Fat: 7g
Fiber: 3g
Carbohydrates: 5g
Protein: 3g

2.   CHEDDAR AND BROCCOLI BAKE

Preparation Time: 5 minutes
Cooking Time: 25 minutes
Servings: 2
Ingredients:

- Broccoli head, florets separated and roughly chopped
- 2 oz. cheddar cheese, grated
- 4 eggs, whisked
- 1 cup almond milk
- 2 tsp. cilantro, chopped
- Salt and black pepper to the taste

Directions:
1.   In a bowl, put and mix the eggs with the milk, cilantro, salt and pepper and whisk.
2.   Put the broccoli in your air fryer, add the eggs mix over it, spread, sprinkle the cheese on top, cook

350°F for 25 minutes, divide between plates and serve for breakfast.
Nutrition:
Calories 214
Fat 14g
Fiber 2g
Carbohydrates 4g
Protein 9g

3.   BASIL MOZZARELLA EGGS

Preparation Time: 5 minutes
Cooking Time: 20 minutes
Servings: 2
Ingredients:

- 2 tbsp. butter, melted
- 6 tsp. basil pesto
- 1 cup mozzarella cheese, grated
- 6 eggs, whisked
- 2 tbsp. basil, chopped
- A pinch of salt and black pepper

Directions:
1.   In a bowl, put and combine all the ingredients except the butter and whisk them well.
2.   Preheat your Air Fryer at 360°F, drizzle the butter on the bottom, spread the eggs mix, cook for 20 minutes, and serve for breakfast.

Nutrition:
Calories 207
Fat 14g
Fiber 3g
Carbohydrates 4g
Protein 8g

4.   WHOLESOME KETO AVO-BURGERS

Preparation Time: 5 minutes
Cooking Time: 5 minutes
Servings: 2
Ingredients:

- 2 avocados
- 2 eggs

- 2 tbsp. chopped lettuce
- 2 tbsp. mayonnaise
- 4 strips of bacon

Directions:

1. Bring out a skillet pan, put it over medium heat and when hot, add bacon strips and cook for 5 minutes until crispy.
2. Put bacon to a plate lined with paper towels, crack an egg into the pan, and cook for at least 2 to 4 minutes, until fried to the desired level; fry remaining egg in the same manner.
3. Prepare sandwiches and for this, cut each avocado in half widthwise, remove the pit, and scoop out the flesh.
4. Fill the hollow of two avocado halves with mayonnaise, then top each half with 1 tablespoon of chopped lettuce, 2 bacon strips, and a fried egg, and then cover with the second half of avocado.
5. Sprinkle sesame seeds on avocados and serve.

Nutrition:
Calories: 205
Fats: 19g
Protein: 8g
Carbohydrates: 1g

5. CHEESY BRUSSELS SPROUTS AND EGGS

Preparation Time: 5 minutes
Cooking Time: 20 minutes
Servings: 2
Ingredients:

- 1 tbsp. olive oil
- 1 lb. Brussels sprouts, shredded
- 4 eggs, whisked
- ½-cup coconut cream
- Salt and black pepper to the taste
- 1 tbsp chives, chopped
- ¼ cup cheddar cheese, shredded

Directions:

1. Preheat the Air Fryer at 360°F and grease it with the oil.
2. Spread the Brussels sprouts on the bottom of the fryer, then add the eggs mixed with the rest of the ingredients, toss a bit and cook for 20 minutes.
3. Divide between plates and serve.

Nutrition:
Calories 242

Fat 12g
Fiber 3g
Carbohydrates 5g
Protein 9g

6. EGGS IN PEPPER

Preparation Time: 20 minutes
Cooking Time: 6 minutes
Servings: 2
Ingredients:

- 6 eggs
- 1 bell pepper, sliced into ¼ in. rings
- Salt and ground black pepper, to taste
- 2 tbsp. of chopped chives and parsley
- 2 tbsp. of olive oil

Directions:

1. Heat a frying pan to medium heat temperature and grease it lightly.
2. Place bell pepper rings in the pan for 2 minutes.
3. Flip the rings and crack an egg in the middle of the rings.
4. Add salt and pepper.
5. Cook 2-4 minutes.
6. Repeat with other pepper rings and eggs.
7. Garnish with parsley and chives.

Nutrition:
Calories: 157
Total Fats: 12g
Net Carbs: 6g
Protein: 12g
Fiber: 6.3g

7. NAAN BREAD AND BUTTER

Preparation Time: 20 minutes
Cooking Time: 5 minutes
Servings: 2
Ingredients:

- 7 tbsp. coconut oil
- ¾ cup coconut flour
- 2 tablespoons psyllium powder
- ½ tsp. baking powder
- Salt, to taste
- 2 cups hot water
- Some coconut oil, for frying
- 2 garlic cloves, peeled and minced
- 3. 5 oz. butter

Directions:

1.	In a bowl, combine the coconut flour with baking powder, salt, and psyllium powder, and stir.
2.	Add the coconut oil and the hot water and knead the dough. Set aside for 5 minutes, divide into 6 balls, and flatten them on a working surface.
3.	In a pan, pour coconut oil the heat it over medium-high heat, add the naan bread to the pan, fry it until golden brown then transfer them to a plate.
4.	Heat up a pan with the butter over medium-high heat, add the garlic, salt, and pepper, stir, and cook for 2 minutes.
5.	Brush the naan bread with this mixture, pour the rest into a bowl, and serve.
Nutrition:
Calories: 140
Total Fats: 9g
Net Carbs: 3g
Protein: 4g
Fiber: 1g

## 8.	BREAKFAST TUNA SALAD

Preparation Time: 10 minutes
Cooking Time: 4 minutes
Servings: 2
Ingredients:
•	2 tbsp. of sour cream
•	12 oz. of canned tuna in olive oil
•	4 leeks, diced
•	A pinch of red chili flakes
•	1 tbsp. of capers
•	8 tbsp. of mayonnaise
•	Salt and ground black pepper, to taste
Directions:
1.	Mix all ingredients listed in one salad bowl.
2.	Stir well and serve.
Nutrition:
Calories: 160g
Total Fats: 3g
Net Carbs: 2g
Protein: 6g
Fiber: 1g

## 9.	LOW-CARB MUFFINS WITH WHEY

Preparation Time: 10 minutes
Cooking Time: 30 minutes
Servings: 2
Ingredients:

•	1 egg
•	4 tsp. of whey (Chocolate)
•	4 tbsp. of low-fat milk
•	1 tsp. of cacao
•	½ tsp. of vanilla sugar
•	½ pack of baking powder
Directions:
1.	In one bowl, whisk 1 egg with milk and vanilla sugar. Combine them well.
2.	Gradually, add whey, cacao, and baking powder to the mixture. Mix constantly.
3.	Pour resulting mixture into muffin molds.
4.	Bake at 220°F for 30 minutes. Enjoy!
Nutrition:
Calories: 112
Total Fats: 5g
Net Carbs: 6g
Protein: 1.2g
Fiber: 3.3g

## 10.	SPINACH ROLLS

Preparation Time: 10 minutes
Cooking Time: 10 minutes
Servings: 2
Ingredients:
•	7 oz. of white meat, cut into small cubes
•	1 cup of spinach
•	4 eggs
•	7 oz. of cream cheese
•	1 tbsp. of sesame seeds
•	½ tsp. of sodium bicarbonate
•	4 tbsp. of flour
Directions:
1.	Cook spinach and meat in water. (Separately)
2.	Whisk 3 eggs with 4 tbsp. of flour, sodium, salt, and 2 tbsp. of cheese and ½ cup of cooked spinach.
3.	Mix them well and bake at 250°F for 10 minutes.
4.	Meanwhile, dissolve a pinch of salt in water. Add ½ cup of cooked spinach, meat and 1 egg. Cook the mixture in a cooking pot until meat is done.
5.	Cut baked dough into smaller sizes, fill them with cooked mixture and roll. Enjoy!
Nutrition:
Calories: 123
Total Fats: 4g

Net Carbs: 8g
Protein: 3g
Fiber: 2.4g

11.   PESTO SCRAMBLE

Preparation Time: 5 minutes
Cooking Time: 5 minutes
Servings: 2
Ingredients:

- 1 tbsp. basil pesto
- 1 tbsp. unsalted butter
- 1/8 tsp ground black pepper
- 1/8 tsp salt
- 2 eggs
- 2 tbsp. grated cheddar cheese

Directions:
1.   Crack eggs in a bowl, add cheese, black pepper, salt, and pesto and whisk until combined.
2.   Bring out a skillet pan, put it over medium heat, add the butter and when it melts, add in the egg mixture and cook for 3 to 5 min until eggs have scrambled to the desired level.
Nutrition:
Calories: 160
Fats: 7g
Protein: 2g
Carbohydrates: 0g

12.   CHEESY TURKEY BAKE

Preparation Time: 5 minutes
Cooking Time: 25 minutes
Servings: 2
Ingredients:

- 1 turkey breast, skinless, boneless, cut into strips and browned
- 2 tsp. olive oil
- 2 cups almond milk
- 2 cups cheddar cheese, shredded

- 2 eggs, whisked
- Salt and black pepper to the taste
- 1 tbsp. chives, chopped

Directions:
1.   In a bowl, mix the eggs with milk, cheese, salt, pepper, and the chives and whisk well.
2.   Preheat the air fryer at 330°F, add the oil, heat it, add the turkey pieces, and spread them well.
3.   Add the egg mixture, toss a bit, and cook for 25 minutes.
4.   Serve right away for breakfast.
Nutrition:
Calories: 244
Fat: 11g
Fiber: 4g
Carbohydrates: 5g
Protein: 7g

13.   TOMATOES AND EGGS MIX

Preparation Time: 5 minutes
Cooking Time: 25 minutes
Servings: 2
Ingredients:

- 1½ tbsp. olive oil
- 30 oz. canned tomatoes, chopped
- ½ lb. cheddar, shredded
- 2 tbsp. chives, chopped
- Salt and black pepper to the taste
- 6 eggs, whisked

Directions:
1.   Put the oil in air fryer, heat it at 350°F, add the tomatoes, eggs, salt, and pepper and whisk.

2. Add the cheese on top and sprinkle the chives on top.
3. Cook for around 25 minutes, divide between plates and serve for breakfast.
Nutrition:
Calories: 221
Fat: 8g
Fiber: 3g
Carbohydrates: 4g
Protein: 8g

14. CREAMY ALMOND AND CHEESE MIX

Preparation Time: 10 minutes
Cooking Time: 20 minutes
Servings: 2
Ingredients:
- 1-cup almond milk
- Cooking spray
- 9 oz. cream cheese, soft
- 1 cup cheddar cheese, shredded
- 6 spring onions, chopped
- Salt and black pepper to the taste
- 6 eggs, whisked

Directions:
1. Heat up your air fryer with the oil at 350°F and grease it with cooking spray.
2. In a bowl, put and mixed the eggs with the rest of the ingredients, whisk well, pour and spread into the air fryer and cook everything for 20 minutes.
3. Divide everything between plates and serve.
Nutrition:
Calories 231
Fat 11g
Fiber 3g
Carbohydrates 5g
Protein 8g

15. OLIVES BAKE

Preparation Time: 5 minutes
Cooking Time: 20 minutes
Servings: 2
Ingredients:
- 2 cups black olives, pitted and chopped
- 4 eggs, whisked
- ¼-tsp. sweet paprika
- 1 tbsp. cilantro, chopped
- ½ cup cheddar, shredded
- A pinch of salt and black pepper
- Cooking spray

Directions:
1. In a bowl, put and mix the eggs with the olives and all the ingredients except the cooking spray and stir well.
2. Heat the air fryer at 350°F, grease it with cooking spray, pour the olives and eggs mixture, spread and cook for 20 minutes.
3. Divide between plates and serve for breakfast.
Nutrition:
Calories 240
Fat 14g
Fiber 3g
Carbohydrates 5g
Protein 8g

16. CLASSIC STEAK 'N EGGS

Preparation Time: 5 minutes
Cooking Time: 15 minutes
Servings: 2
Ingredients:
- 8 eggs
- 16 oz. sirloin steak
- 4 tbsp. butter
- 1 ripe avocado
- Salt and pepper to taste

Directions:
1. Melt 2 tablespoon of butter in a huge skillet.
2. Fry eggs 4 at a time until the edges are crispy.
3. While the second batch of eggs are cooking, cook the sirloin in another skillet (with the other 2 tablespoons of butter) until it's at least 160°F.
4. Season eggs and steak well with salt and pepper.
5. Serve with slices of avocado.

Nutrition:
Total calories: 480
Protein: 37g
Carbs: 4g
Fat: 37g
Fiber: 3g

17. HOMEMADE SAUSAGE, EGG, AND CHEESE SANDWICH

Preparation Time: 5 minutes
Cooking Time: 30 minutes
Servings: 1
Ingredients:
Muffin
- 1 egg
- 1 tbsp. coconut flour
- 1 tbsp. almond milk
- ½ tbsp. olive oil
- ½-tsp. baking powder
- Pinch of salt

Filling
- 1 egg
- ¼-lb. breakfast sausage
- 1 slice cheddar cheese

Directions:
1. Preheat oven to 400°F.
2. Begin by mixing your muffin batter together first by cracking an egg in a bowl, then mixing in the rest of the ingredients.
3. Grease a ramekin and pour in the batter.
4. Bake for 15 minutes.
5. To get an egg that's the same size as your muffin, crack an egg in a ramekin and whisk.
6. Flavor with salt and pepper, then bake for 10 minutes.
7. For your sausage, just form the meat into a patty.
8. Heat a skillet, and then cook patty for 4-5 minutes per side.

9. When the muffins are ready, remove from oven and carefully slice them in half.

10. For a toasty muffin, stick in a toaster for a few minutes.

11. Build sandwich and top with a slice of cheese.

12. Eat!

Nutrition:

Total calories: 460

Protein: 29g

Carbs: 3g

Fat: 37g

Fiber: 0g

18. CHICKEN SAUSAGE BREAKFAST CASSEROLE

Preparation Time: 10 minutes

Cooking Time: 40 minutes

Servings: 2

Ingredients:

- 1 lb. chicken sausage
- 3 big eggs
- 2 cups chopped tomatoes
- 2 cups diced zucchini
- 1 ½ cups cheddar cheese
- ½ cup diced onion
- ½ cup plain Greek yogurt
- 1 tsp. dried sage
- 1 tsp. dried mustard

Directions:

1. Preheat oven to 375°F.

2. Preheat a skillet until warm, then add sausage.

3. When nearly all the pink is gone, put the zucchini and onion.

4. Cook until the veggies are softened.

5. Move skillet contents to a greased casserole dish.

6. In a separate bowl, mix eggs, yogurt, and seasonings together.

7. Lastly, mix one cup of cheese into eggs.

8. Pour into the casserole dish on top of the sausage and veggies.

9. Bake for at least 30 minutes until cheese has melted and starts browning.

10. Serve right away!

Nutrition:

Calories: 487

Protein: 19g

Carbs: 4.8g

Fat: 42g

Fiber: 1.3g

19. CHEDDAR-CHIVE OMELET FOR ONE

Preparation Time: 8 minutes

Cooking Time: 5 minutes

Servings: 1

Ingredients:

- 2 slices cooked bacon
- 2 big eggs
- 2 stalks chives
- 2 tbsp. sharp cheddar cheese
- 1 tsp. olive oil
- Salt and pepper to taste

Directions:

1. Heat oil in a skillet.

2. While that heats, chop chives.

3.   Pour in eggs and sprinkle chives, salt, and pepper on top.
4.   Wait until edges are beginning to set.
5.   Crumble bacon on top and wait another 25 seconds.
6.   Remove skillet from heat.
7.   Sprinkle on cheese and carefully fold omelet over.
8.   Enjoy!

Nutrition:
Calories: 463
Protein: 24g
Carbs: 1g
Fat: 39g
Fiber: 1g

20.   BREAKFAST-STUFFED   BELL PEPPERS

Preparation Time: 25 minutes
Cooking Time: 10 minutes
Servings: 2
Ingredients:
- 4 large yellow bell peppers
- 4 eggs
- 4 bacon strips
- 4 oz. pork breakfast sausage
- 1 cup shredded mozzarella cheese
- ½ cup diced onion
- 1 tbsp. minced garlic
- Couple teaspoons olive oil
- Salt and pepper to taste

Directions:
1.   Preheat your oven to 275°F.
2.   Chop the tops off the peppers and hollow out the insides.
3.   Set on a baking sheet and brush insides with a little olive oil.
4.   Stick peppers in the oven.
5.   Heat a skillet and cook bacon and sausage until nearly done.
6.   Add onions and garlic.
7.   Cook until onions have softened.
8.   Take out the peppers and stuff.
9.   Top with cheese and press down with a spoon, creating a little hollow.
10.   Crack in an egg.
11.   Turn oven up to 325°F and put stuffed peppers in the oven for 10 minutes, or until eggs have reached the doneness you like.
12.   Serve!

Nutrition:
Calories: 372
Protein: 27g
Carbs: 1g
Fat: 24g
Fiber: 2g

21.   FRIED   CODFISH   WITH ALMONDS

Preparation Time: 8 minutes
Cooking Time: 18 minutes
Servings: 2
Ingredients:
- 16 oz. codfish fillet
- 3 oz. chopped almonds
- ½ tsp chili pepper
- 1 egg
- 1 tbsp. ghee butter
- 1 tsp psyllium
- 3 oz. cream
- 3 tbsp. keto mayo
- 1 tbsp. chopped fresh dill
- 1 tsp minced garlic
- ½ tsp onion powder
- Salt and pepper to taste

Directions:
1.   In a small mixing bowl, combine the psyllium, onion powder, chili, and almonds

2.   Beat the eggs in another bowl, mix well
3.   Warm the butter in a skillet at medium heat.
4.   Cut the fillet into 3 slices
5.   Dip into the egg mixture, then into almonds and spices
6.   Fry in the skillet for about 7 minutes each side
7.   Meanwhile, in another bowl combine the cream, garlic, dill, and salt, stir well
8.   Serve the fish with this sauce

Nutrition:
Carbs: 4.9 g
Fats: 63 g
Protein: 33.6 g
Calories: 709

22.   SALMON BALLS

Preparation Time: 5 minutes
Cooking Time: 13 minutes
Servings: 2
Ingredients:
- 1 can of tuna
- 2 tbsp. keto mayo
- 1 avocado
- 1 egg
- 1 garlic clove
- ½ cup heavy cream
- 3 tbsp. coconut oil
- ½ tsp ginger powder
- ½ tsp paprika
- ½ tsp dried cilantro
- 2 tbsp. lemon juice
- 2 tbsp. water
- Salt and ground black pepper to taste

Directions:
1.   Drain the salmon, chop it
2.   Mince the garlic clove, peel the avocado
3.   In a bowl, combine the fish, mayo, egg, and garlic, season with salt, paprika, and ginger, mix well
4.   Make 4 balls of it
5.   Warm the oil in a skillet at medium heat
6.   Put the balls and fry for 4-6 minutes each side
7.   Meanwhile, put the heavy cream, avocado, cilantro, lemon juice, and 1 tablespoon of oil in a blender. Pulse well
8.   Serve the balls with the sauce

Nutrition:

Carbs: 3.9 g
Fats: 50 g
Protein: 20.1 g
Calories: 555

23.   SHRIMP RISOTTO

Preparation Time: 10 minutes
Cooking Time: 15 minutes
Servings: 2
Ingredients:
- 14 oz. shrimps, peeled and deveined
- 12 oz. cauli rice
- 4 button mushrooms
- ½ lemon
- 4 stalks green onion
- 3 tbsp. ghee butter
- 2 tbsp. coconut oil
- Salt and black pepper to taste

Directions:
1.   Preheat the oven to 400F
2.   Put a layer of cauli rice on a sheet pan, season with salt and spices; sprinkle the coconut oil over it
3.   Bake in the oven for 10-12 minutes
4.   Cut the green onion, slice up the mushrooms and remove the rind from the lemon
5.   Heat the ghee butter in a skillet over medium heat. Add the shrimps; season it and sauté for 5-6 minutes
6.   Top the cauli rice with the shrimps, sprinkle the green onion over it

Nutrition:
Carbs: 9.2 g
Fat: 26, 2 g
Protein: 25 g
Calories: 363

24.   LEMONY TROUT

Preparation Time: 10 minutes
Cooking Time: 20 minutes
Servings: 2
Ingredients:
- 5 tbsp. ghee butter
- 5 oz. trout fillets
- 2 garlic cloves
- 1 tsp rosemary
- 1 lemon
- 2 tbsp. capers

- Salt and pepper to taste

Directions:

1. Preheat the oven to 400F
2. Peel the lemon, mince the garlic cloves and chop the capers
3. Season the trout fillets with salt, rosemary, and pepper
4. Grease a baking dish with the oil and place the fish onto it
5. Warm the butter in a skillet over medium heat
6. Add the garlic and cook for 4-5 minutes until golden
7. Remove from the heat, add the lemon zest and 2 tablespoons of lemon juice, stir well
8. Pour the lemon-butter sauce over the fish and top with the capers
9. Bake for 14-15 minutes. Serve hot

Nutrition:

Carbs: 3.1 g
Fat: 25 g
Protein: 15, 8 g
Calories: 302

25. ROASTED WHOLE CHICKEN

Preparation Time: 20 minutes
Cooking Time: 1 and 32 minutes
Servings: 2
Ingredients:

- 10 tbsp. unsalted butter
- 3 garlic cloves, minced
- 1 (3-lb.) grass-fed whole chicken, neck, and giblets removed
- Salt and ground black pepper, as required

Directions:

1. Preheat the oven to 400ºF. Arrange an oven rack into the lower portion of the oven.
2. Grease a large baking dish.
3. Place the butter and garlic in a small pan over medium heat and cook for about 1-2 minutes.
4. Remove the pan from heat and let it cool for about 2 minutes.
5. Season the inside and outside of chicken evenly with salt and black pepper.
6. Arrange the chicken into a prepared baking dish, breast side up.
7. Pour the garlic butter over and inside of the chicken.

8. Bake for about 1-1½ hours, basting with the pan juices every 20 minutes.
9. Remove from oven and place the chicken onto a cutting board for about 5-10 minutes before carving.
10. Cut into desired size pieces and serve.

Nutrition:

Calories: 772
Fat: 39.1g
Net Carbs: 0.7g
Protein: 99g

26. BUFFALO PIZZA CHICKEN

Preparation Time: 5 minutes
Cooking Time: 5-6 minutes
Servings: 2
Ingredients:

- Vegetable cooking spray
- ½ cup Buffalo-style hot sauce
- 1 (16-oz) package prebaked Italian pizza crust
- 2 cups chopped deli-roasted whole chicken
- 1 cup (4 oz.) shredded Provolone cheese
- ¼ cup crumbled blue cheese

Directions:

1. Coat the grill with the spray and put it on the grill. Preheat grill to 350° F (medium heat).
2. Spread the hot sauce over the crust, and the next 3 ingredients surface.
3. Place the crust on the cooking grate directly. Grill at 350° F (medium heat) for 4 min, covered with the grill lid.
4. Rotate 1-quarter turn pizza and grill, covered with grill top, for 5 to 6 min or until heated thoroughly. Serve right away.

Nutrition:

Calories: 365
Fat: 11g
Net Carbs: 42g
Protein: 24g

27. PORK IN BACON ROLLS

Preparation Time: 15 minutes
Cooking Time: 6 hours
Servings: 2
Ingredients:

- 2 lbs. (907 g.) pork shoulder roast
- 8 bacon strips
- 2 tsp. chopped thyme
- 1 tsp. chopped oregano
- ¼ cup chicken broth
- 3 tbsp. extra-virgin olive oil, divided
- 1 tsp. onion powder
- 1 tsp. garlic powder
- Salt, to taste
- Freshly ground black pepper, to taste

Equipment:
Toothpicks, sock in water for at least 30 minutes
Directions:
1. Coat the insert of a slow cooker with 1 tablespoon olive oil.
2. Put the pork in a large bowl, and sprinkle with onion powder, garlic powder, salt, and black pepper. Toss to coat well.
3. Warm the remaining olive oil in a nonstick skillet over medium-high heat until shimmering.
4. Place the pork in the skillet and roast for 10 minutes or until well browned. Flip the pork halfway through the cooking time. Allow to cool for 10 minutes.
5. Wrap the bacon slices around the pork, securing with a toothpick. Place them in the greased slow cooker, and add the thyme, oregano, and chicken broth.
6. Place the cooker lid on and cook on LOW for 6 hours.
7. Remove the pork from the slow cooker and serve warm.
Nutrition:
Calories: 494
Total fat: 40.2g
Total carbs: 1.1g
Fiber: 0g
Net carbs: 1.1g
Protein: 30.8g

28. BRAISED LAMB

Preparation Time: 10 minutes
Cooking Time: 5 minutes
Servings: 2
Ingredients:

- 8 bone-in lamb chops (about 2 lbs. / 907 g)
- ¼ cup low-carb tomato sauce
- 1 small yellow onion, diced
- 1 cup lamb or beef broth
- 1 tbsp. olive oil
- Salt , to taste
- Freshly ground black pepper, to taste

Directions:
1. Warm the olive oil at medium-high heat in a nonstick skillet until shimmering.
2. Place the lamb chops in a large bowl, and sprinkle with salt and black pepper. Toss to coat well.
3. Put the lamb chops in the skillet and sauté for 2 minutes or until well browned. Flip the lamb chops halfway through the cooking time. Set aside.
4. Add the tomato sauce and onion to the skillet and cook for 2 minutes or until the onion is translucent, then mix in the broth.
5. Place the lamb chops and the tomato sauce mixture in a pressure cooker. Put the lid on and cook for 2 minutes.
6. Release the pressure and transfer the lamb and sauce to a large platter to serve.
Nutrition:
Calories: 352
Total fat: 16.2g
Total carbs: 2.4g
Fiber: 0g
Net carbs: 2.4g
Protein: 47.4g

29. KETO PRIME RIB ROAST WITH GARLIC BUTTER

Preparation Time: 5 minutes
Cooking Time: 2 hours
Servings: 20
Ingredients:

- 1 4-bone standing rib roast
- 2 tbsp. Italian seasoning
- 6 tbsp. butter (melted)
- 1 tsp. black pepper
- 1½ tbsp. sea salt

- 12 cloves garlic (minced)

Directions:

1. Put the prime rib with its fatty side up on a roasting pan with a roasting rack.
2. Season the prime rib liberally with pepper and salt.
3. Let the prime rib rest at room temperature for about an hour.
4. Preheat your oven to 450 °F Fahrenheit.
5. In a mixing bowl, place in the minced garlic, Italian seasoning, and melted butter. Carefully pour it over the prime rib. Spread the mixture evenly on the surface of the prime rib with the use of a basting brush.
6. Put the prime rib in the oven. Roast it for 30 minutes or until the garlic has turned dark golden brown. Make sure that it is not burnt. Cover the top of the prime rib using aluminum foil like a tent.
7. Lower the temperature of the oven to 350°F Fahrenheit. Keep roasting the prime rib until it reaches your desired doneness.
8. Take out the prime rib from the oven. Let the meat rest for about 20 minutes, so it will continue to cook.
9. Carve the roasted prime rib. Serve.

Nutrition:

Calories: 575

Carbs: 0 g

Fats: 51 g

Proteins: 24 g

Fiber: 0 g

30. POTATO CAULIFLOWER LEEK SOUP

Preparation Time: 15 minutes

Cooking Time: 30 minutes

Servings: 2

Ingredients:

- 2 tbsp. olive oil
- 3 leeks, halved lengthwise and chopped
- 4 garlic cloves, minced
- 2 large russet potatoes, peeled and cut into a small dice
- 2 cauliflower heads, cut into small florets (about 5 cups)
- 5 cups classic vegetable broth
- 3 thyme sprigs

- 2 bay leaves
- 1 cup nondairy milk of choice
- Salt
- Black pepper
- 2 tbsp. chopped chives for garnish

Directions:

1. In a large pot, heat the olive oil over medium-high heat. Add the leeks, garlic, and sauté for 3 minutes.
2. Add the potatoes and cauliflower and stir to combine. Add the broth, thyme, and bay leaves and bring to a boil, making sure all the vegetables are fully submerged in the broth. Then reduce the heat and simmer for 25 minutes, until the cauliflower and potatoes are fork tender. Remove the thyme and bay leaves.
3. Using an immersion blender, purée the soup until creamy. Stir in the nondairy milk. If a thinner soup consistency is desired, add more milk or broth and purée until the desired consistency is reached. Alternatively, add the soup to a high-speed blender in small batches to purée.
4. Season with salt and pepper to taste. Garnish with the chives.

Nutrition:

Calories: 250

Fat: 6g

Protein: 9g

Carbohydrates: 43g

Fiber: 7g

31. KETO CHEWY CHAFFLE

Preparation Time: 5 minutes

Cooking Time: 5 minutes

Servings: 2

Ingredients:

- ½ cup shredded mozzarella cheese, full-fat

- 1 egg, pasteurized
- 2 tsp coconut flour

Directions:

1. Turn on a mini waffle maker and let it preheat for 5 minutes.

2. In the meantime, bring out a medium bowl, put all the ingredients in it and then mix by using an immersion blender until smooth.

3. Ladle the batter evenly into the waffle maker, shut with lid, and let it cook for 3 to 4 minutes until firm and golden brown.

Nutrition:

Calories: 142

Fats: 10g

Protein: 3g

Carbohydrates: 1g

32. KETO CREAMY BACON DISH

Preparation Time: 5 minutes

Cooking Time: 7 minutes

Servings: 2

Ingredients:

- ½ tsp dried basil
- ½ tsp minced garlic
- ½ tsp tomato paste
- 2 oz. unsalted butter, softened
- 3 slices of bacon, chopped

Directions:

1. Bring out a skillet pan, put it over medium heat, add 1 tbsp. butter, and when it starts to melts, add chopped bacon and cook for 5 minutes.

2. Then remove the pan from heat, add remaining butter, along with basil and tomato paste,

season with salt and black pepper then stir until well mixed.

3. Move bacon butter into an airtight container, cover with the lid, and refrigerate for 1 hour until solid.

Nutrition:

Calories: 150

Fats: 16g

Protein: 1g

Carbohydrates: 1g

33. EGGPLANT OMELET

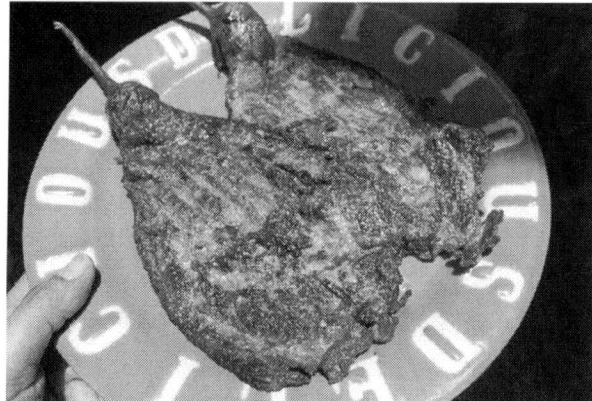

Preparation Time: 5 minutes

Cooking Time: 10 minutes

Servings: 2

Ingredients:

- 1 large eggplant
- 1 tbsp. coconut oil, melted
- 1 tsp. unsalted butter
- 2 eggs
- 2 tbsp. chopped green onions

Directions:

1. Set the grill and let it preheat at the high setting.

2. In the meantime, prepare the eggplant, for this, cut two slices from eggplant, about 1-inch thick, and reserve the remaining eggplant for later use.

3. Brush slices of eggplant with oil, spice with salt on both sides, then put the slices on grill and cook for around 3 to 4 minutes per side.

4. Move grilled eggplant to a cutting board, let it cool for 5 minutes, and then make a home in the center of each slice by using a cookie cutter.

5. Bring out a frying pan, put it over medium heat, add butter and when it melts, add eggplant slices in it and crack an egg into its each hole.

6. Allow the eggs cook for 3 to 4 minutes, then carefully flip the eggplant slice and continue cooking for 3 minutes until the egg has thoroughly cooked.

7. Season egg with salt and black pepper, move them to a plate, then garnish with green onions and serve.

Nutrition:

Calories: 184

Fats: 8g

Protein: 3g

Carbohydrates: 4g

34. KETO LOW CARB CREPE

Preparation Time: 5 minutes

Cooking Time: 8 minutes

Servings: 2

Ingredients:

- 2 eggs
- 1 egg white
- 1 tbsp. unsalted butter
- 1 1/3 tbsp. cream cheese
- 2/3 tbsp. psyllium husk

Directions:

1. Prepare the batter and for this, put all the ingredients in a bowl, except for butter, and then whisk by using a stick blender until smooth and very liquid.

2. Bring out a skillet pan, put it over medium heat, add ½ tbsp. butter and when it melts, pour in half of the batter, spread evenly, and cook until the top has firmed.

3. Carefully flip the crepe, then continue cooking for 2 minutes until cooked and then move it to a plate.

4. Put the remaining butter then when it melts, cook another crepe in the same manner and then serve.

Nutrition:

Calories: 118

Fats: 7g

Protein: 1g

Carbohydrates: 1g

35. KETO CHEESE ROLLS

Preparation Time: 5 minutes

Cooking Time: 0 minutes

Servings: 2

Ingredients:

- 1-oz butter, unsalted
- 2 oz. mozzarella cheese, sliced, full-fat

Directions:

1. Cut cheese into slices and then cut butter into thin slices.

2. Top each cheese slice with a slice of butter, roll it and then serve.

Nutrition:

Calories: 166

Fats: 7gg

Protein: 2g

Carbohydrates: 0g

36. AVOCADO STUFFED WITH TUNA

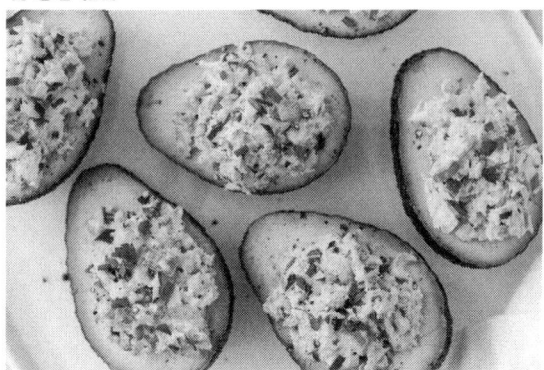

Preparation Time: 20 minutes
Cooking Time: 0 minutes
Servings: 2
Ingredients:
- 1 avocado
- 1 can of tuna
- 1 tomato
- ½ onion
- Parsley to taste

Directions:
1. Cut the avocado into halves. Remove the middle parts so that you can have a room for stuffing. (Keep the "meat" parts)
2. Cut the tomato and onion into tiny circles.
3. Mix meat parts with tuna, tomato, and onion.
4. Stuff the avocado halves with the mixture, decorate with parsley to taste and serve!

Nutrition:
Calories: 132
Fats: 3g
Net Carbs: 6g
Protein: 1.2g
Fiber: 7g

37. TUNA IN CUCUMBER

Preparation Time: 15 minutes
Cooking Time: 0 minutes
Servings: 2
Ingredients:
- 1 cucumber
- ½ celery leaf
- ½ red bell pepper
- 1 can of tuna
- Pepper and salt to taste

Directions:
1. Peel the cucumber and cut it into thicker circles. Make a hole in each piece.
2. Cut the celery and pepper into tiny cubes. Mix them with tuna.
3. Put 1 tbsp. of tuna mixture into cucumbers.
4. Add spices to taste and serve.
5. Enjoy!

Nutrition:
Calories: 109
Total Fats: 1.6g
Net Carbs: 4g
Protein: 1g
Fiber: 5.4g

38. SMALL KETO PIES

S

Preparation Time: 10 minutes
Cooking Time: 30 minutes
Servings: 2
Ingredients:
- 3 eggs
- 5 bacon slices
- ½ red bell pepper
- 1 leek
- ½ cup of broccoli
- 2 oz. of ground cheese
- ½ cup of yogurt
- ¼ pack of baking powder
- 2 tbsp. of olive oil
- Salt, pepper, powdered garlic, parsley to taste

Directions:
1. Whisk and blend the eggs with baking powder.
2. Cook the broccoli in water.
3. Cut bacon, leek and pepper into smaller pieces to taste.
4. Mix cheese with yogurt well. Then, add bacon, leek, pepper, and spices to taste.
5. Join the 2 mixtures together and then pour into cupcake or muffin molds.
6. Bake for 30 minutes at 200°F.

Nutrition:
Calories: 121
Total Fats: 2.1g
Net Carbs: 2g
Protein: 1.3g
Fiber: 6g

39. KETO WRAPS

Preparation Time: 30 minutes
Cooking Time: 0 minutes
Servings: 2
Ingredients:
- 10 oz. of turkey meat
- 3 oz. of bacon
- 1 tomato
- 3 oz. of mozzarella
- Cabbage leaves for wrapping

For coating:
- 1 cup of mayonnaise
- 6 basil leaves
- 1 tsp. of lemon juice
- 1 tsp. of powdered garlic
- 1 tsp. of salt
- 1 tsp. of pepper

Directions:
1. Mix all ingredients listed for coating in one bowl. You should get a dense mixture.
2. Prepare bacon in a frying pan.
3. Coat cabbage leaves with coating mixture. Pile ingredients over (turkey, tomatoes, bacon and cheese).
4. Wrap the cabbage like tortillas and serve.

Nutrition:
Calories: 121
Total Fats: 6.9g
Net Carbs: 4g
Protein: 2.4g
Fiber: 5.6g

40. CHICKEN OMELET

Preparation Time: 5 minutes
Cooking Time: 10 minutes
Servings: 2
Ingredients:

- 1 oz. of rotisserie chicken, shredded
- 1 tsp. of mustard
- 1 tbsp. of mayonnaise
- 1 tomato, cored and chopped
- 2 bacon slices, cooked and crumbled
- 2 eggs
- 1 small avocado, pitted, peeled and chopped
- Salt and ground black pepper, to taste

Directions:
1.   Heat up a pan over medium heat, grease lightly with cooking oil.
2.   Mix the eggs with some salt and pepper in a bowl and whisk.
3.   Add the eggs in the pan and cook the omelet for 5 minutes.
4.   Add the chicken, avocado, tomato, bacon, mayonnaise and mustard on one half of the omelet.
5.   Fold the omelet, cover pan, cook for 5 minutes and serve.
Nutrition:
Calories: 400
Total Fats: 32g
Net Carbs: 4g
Protein: 25g
Fiber: 6g

41. SAVORY HAM AND CHEESE WAFFLES

Preparation Time: 10 minutes
Cooking Time: 10 minutes
Servings: 2
Ingredients:

- 2 oz. (57 g) ham steak, chopped
- 2 oz. (57 g) Cheddar cheese, grated
- 8 eggs
- 1 tsp. baking powder
- Basil, to taste

From the cupboard:

- 12 tbsp. butter, melted
- Olive oil, as needed
- 1-tsp. sea salt
- Special Equipment:
- A waffle iron

Directions:
1.   Preheat the waffle iron and set aside.
2.   Crack the eggs and keep the egg yolks and egg whites in two separate bowls.
3.   Add the butter, baking powder, basil, and salt to the egg yolks. Whisk well. Fold in the chopped ham and stir until well combined. Set aside.
4.   Lightly season the egg whites with salt and beat until it forms stiff peaks.
5.   Add the egg whites into the bowl of egg yolk mixture. Allow to sit for about 5 minutes.
6.   Lightly coat the waffle iron with the olive oil. Slowly pour half of the mixture in the waffle iron and cook for about 4 minutes. Repeat with the remaining egg mixture.
7.   Take off from the waffle iron and serve warm on two serving plates.

Nutrition:
Calories: 636
Fat: 50.2g
Protein: 45.1g
Net carbs: 1.1g

42. CLASSIC SPANAKOPITA FRITTATA

Preparation Time: 10 minutes
Cooking Time: 3-4 hours
Servings: 2
Ingredients:
- 12 eggs, beaten
- ½ cup feta cheese
- 1 cup heavy whipping cream
- 2 cups spinach, chopped
- 2 tsp. garlic, minced

From the cupboard:
- 1 tablespoon extra-virgin olive oil

Directions:
1. Grease the bottom of the slow cooker, put with the olive oil lightly.
2. Stir together the beaten eggs, feta cheese, heavy cream, spinach, and garlic until well combined.
3. Slowly pour the mixture into the slow cooker. Cook covered on LOW for 3 to 4 hours, or until a knife inserted in the center comes out clean.
4. Take off from the slow cooker and cool for about 3 minutes before slicing.

Nutrition:
Calories: 254
Fat: 22.3g
Protein: 11.1g
Net carbs: 2.1g
Fiber: 0g

43. SAUSAGE STUFFED BELL PEPPERS

Preparation Time: 15 minutes
Cooking Time: 4-5 hours
Servings: 2
Ingredients:
- 1 cup breakfast sausage, crumbled
- 4 bell peppers, seedless and cut the top
- ½ cup coconut milk
- 6 eggs
- 1 cup cheddar cheese, shredded

From the cupboard:
- 1 tbsp. extra-virgin olive oil
- ½ tsp. freshly ground black pepper

Directions:
1. Add the coconut milk, eggs, and black pepper in a medium bowl, whisking until smooth. Set aside.
2. Line your slow cooker insert with aluminum foil. Grease the aluminum foil with 1 tablespoon olive oil.
3. Evenly stuff four bell peppers with the crumbled sausage, and spoon the egg mixture into the peppers.
4. Arrange the stuffed peppers in the slow cooker. Sprinkle the cheese on top.
5. Cook covered on LOW for 4 t0 5 hours, or until the peppers are browned and the eggs are completely set.
6. Divide in 4 serving plates and serve warm.

Nutrition:
Calories: 459
Fat: 36.3g
Protein: 25.2g
Net carbs: 7.9g Fiber: 3g

44. PUMPKIN MUFFINS WITH ALMOND MILK

Preparation Time: 10 minutes
Cooking Time: 30 minutes
Servings: 2
Ingredients:

- ½ cup pumpkin, pitted and diced
- ½ cup unsweetened almond milk
- ¼ cup ground flaxseeds
- 1 cup almond flour
- ½ tsp. vanilla extract

From the cupboard

- ¼ cup coconut oil
- ¼ tsp. stevia

Special Equipment:

- A 12-cup muffin pan

Directions:
1. Set the oven to 350°F. Line a muffin pan using 12 paper liners and set aside.
2. Blend the coconut oil, stevia, pumpkin, almond milk, flaxseeds, almond flour, and vanilla extract in a blender until it forms a smooth batter.
3. Evenly divide the batter into the 12 paper liners. Arrange the muffin pan in the preheated oven and bake until a toothpick inserted in the center comes out clean, for about 3o minutes.
4. Remove from the oven and cool for 8 minutes before serving.

Nutrition:
Calories: 120
Fat: 11.2g
Protein: 3.2g
Net carbs: 1.7g Fiber: 1.9g

45. KETO TACOS WITH GUACAMOLE AND BACON

Preparation Time: 5 minutes
Cooking Time: 10 minutes
Servings: 2
Ingredients:

- 1/4 cup organic romaine lettuce (chopped)
- 3 tbsp. organic sweet potatoes (diced and cooked)
- 1 tbsp. Brain Octane Oil
- 1 tbsp. ghee (grass-fed)
- 2 pieces eggs (pasture-raised)
- 1 piece medium avocado (organic)
- 2 slices pastured bacon (cooked)
- 1/4 tsp. Himalayan pink salt
- organic micro cilantro (for garnish)

Directions:
1. In a skillet over medium heat, heat up the ghee.
2. Get an egg. Crack the egg in the middle of the skillet. Poke the egg yolk.
3. Let the egg cook until solid for about 2 minutes per side. Transfer the cooked egg onto a plate lined with paper towels to absorb the excess oil.
4. Cook the other egg in a similar way. The 2 cooked eggs will serve as the taco shells.
5. In a mixing bowl, put in the avocado, pink salt, and octane oil. Mash the avocado and mix well.
6. Equally divide the avocado mixture into 2 portions. Spread each avocado mixture onto each egg taco.
7. Arrange the romaine lettuce on top of each taco shell.
8. Put a bacon slice on each taco. Top each taco with the cooked sweet potatoes.
9. Garnish the tacos with micro cilantro and sprinkle some pink salt for added taste.

10.   Fold each taco in half. Serve.
Nutrition:
Calories: 387
Carbs: 9 g
Fats: 35 g
Proteins: 11 g
Fiber: 5 g

46.   CHEESE OMELET

Preparation Time: 5 minutes
Cooking Time: 10 minutes
Servings: 2
Ingredients:

- 6 eggs
- 3 oz. ghee
- 7 oz. shredded cheddar cheese
- salt and pepper

Directions:

1.   Whisk the eggs until smooth. Compound half of the cheese and season it with salt and pepper.
2.   Melt the butter in a pan. Pour in the mixture and let it sit for a few minutes (3-4)
3.   When the mixture is looking good, add the other half of the cheese. Serve immediately.

Nutrition:
Carbs: 4 g;
Fat: 80 g;
Protein: 40 g;
Calories: 897 kcal

47.   CHICKEN WITH LEMON PARSLEY BUTTER

Preparation Time: 10 minutes
Cooking Time: 3 hours
Servings: 2
Ingredients:

- 1 (5 – 6lbs) whole roasting chicken, rinsed
- 1 cup of water
- 1/2 tsp. of kosher salt
- 1/4 tsp. of black pepper
- 1 whole lemon, sliced
- 4 tablespoons of butter
- 2 tsp. of fresh parsley, chopped

Directions:
1. Start by seasoning the chicken with all the herbs and spices.
2. Place this chicken in the Crockpot.
3. Cover it and cook for 3 hours on High Settings.
4. Meanwhile, melt butter with lemon slices and parsley in a saucepan.
5. Drizzle the butter over the Crockpot chicken.
6. Serve warm.

Nutrition:
Calories 379
Total Fat 29.7 g
Saturated Fat 18.6 g
Cholesterol 141 mg
Total Carbs 9.7g
Fiber 0.9 g
Sugar 1.3 g
Sodium 193 mg
Potassium 131 mg
Protein 25.2 g
Net Carbs: 5.6g

48.   PAPRIKA CHICKEN

Preparation Time: 10 minutes
Cooking Time: 8 hours
Servings: 2
Ingredients:

- 1 free-range whole chicken
- 1 tbsp. of olive oil
- 1 tbsp. of dried paprika
- 1 tbsp. of curry powder
- 1 tsp. of dried turmeric
- 1 tsp. of salt

Directions:
1. Start by mixing all the spices and oil in a bowl except chicken.
2. Now season the chicken with these spices liberally.
3. Add the chicken and spices to your Crockpot.
4. Cover the lid of the crockpot and cook for 8 hours on Low.
5. Serve warm.

Nutrition:
Calories 313
Total Fat 134g
Saturated Fat 78 g
Cholesterol 861 mg
Total Carbs 6.3 g
Net Carbs: 1.8g

49.   ROTISSERIE CHICKEN

Preparation Time: 10 minutes
Cooking Time: 8 hours 5 minutes
Servings: 2
Ingredients:

- 1 organic whole chicken
- 1 tbsp. of olive oil
- 1 tsp. of thyme
- 1 tsp. of rosemary
- 1 tsp. of garlic, granulated
- salt and pepper

Directions:
1. Start by seasoning the chicken with all the herbs and spices.
2. Broil this seasoned chicken for 5 minutes in the oven until golden brown.
3. Place this chicken in the Crockpot.
4. Cover it and cook for 8 hours on Low Settings.
5. Serve warm.

Nutrition:
Calories 301
Total Fat 12.2 g
Saturated Fat 2.4 g
Polyunsaturated 2.6g
Saturated fats 12g
Monounsaturated fats 2.6g
Polyunsaturated fats 1.4g
Total carbs 10g
Net carbs 4.2g
Protein 28.8 g

50. CROCKPOT CHICKEN ADOBO

Preparation Time: 10 minutes
Cooking Time: 8 hours
Servings: 2
Ingredients:

- 1/4 cup of apple cider vinegar
- 12 chicken drumsticks
- 1 onion, diced into slices
- 2 tbsp. of olive oil
- 10 cloves garlic, smashed
- 1 cup of gluten-free tamari
- 1/4 cup of diced green onion

Directions:
1.   Place the drumsticks in the Crockpot and then add the remaining Ingredients: on top.
2.   Cover it and cook for 8 hours on Low Settings.
3.   Mix gently, then serve warm.

Nutrition:
Calories 249
Total Fat 11.9 g
Polyunsaturated 2.6g
Monounsaturated fats 2.6g
Polyunsaturated fats 1.4g
Net carbs 4.2g
Saturated Fat 1.7 g
Cholesterol 78 mg
Total Carbs 1.8 g

51. CHICKEN GINGER CURRY

Preparation Time: 10 minutes
Cooking Time: 6 hours
Servings: 2
Ingredients:

- 1 ½ lbs. chicken drumsticks (approx. 5 drumsticks), skin removed
- 1 (13.5 g) can coconut milk
- 1 onion, diced
- 4 cloves garlic, minced
- 1-inch knob fresh ginger, minced
- 1 Serrano pepper, minced
- 1 tbsp. of Garam Masala
- ½ tsp. of cayenne
- ½ tsp. of paprika
- ½ tsp. of turmeric
- salt and pepper, adjust to taste

Directions:
1.   Start by throwing all the Ingredients: into the Crockpot.
2.   Cover it and cook for 6 hours on Low Settings.
3.   Garnish as desired.
4.   Serve warm.

Nutrition:
Calories 248
Total Fat 15.7 g
Saturated Fat 2.7 g
Polyunsaturated 2.6g
Monounsaturated fats 2.6g
Polyunsaturated fats 1.4g
Total carbs 10g
Net carbs 4.2g

52. THAI CHICKEN CURRY

Preparation Time: 10 minutes
Cooking Time: 2.5 hours
Servings: 2
Ingredients:

- 1 can coconut milk
- 1/2 cup of chicken stock
- 1 lb. boneless, skinless chicken thighs, diced
- 1 2 tbsp. of red curry paste
- 1 tbsp. of coconut aminos
- 1 tbsp. of fish sauce
- 3 garlic cloves, minced
- Salt and black pepper-to taste
- red pepper flakes as desired
- 1 bag frozen mixed veggies

Directions:
1.   Start by throwing all the Ingredient except vegetables into the Crockpot.
2.   Cover it and cook for 2 hours on Low Settings.
3.   Remove its lid and thawed veggies.
4.   Cover the crockpot again then continue cooking for another 30 minutes on Low settings.
5.   Garnish as desired.
6.   Serve warm.

Nutrition:
Calories 327
Total Fat 3.5 g
Saturated Fat 0.5 g
Cholesterol 162 mg

Total Carbs 56g
Net Carbs: 24g

53. LEMONGRASS AND COCONUT CHICKEN DRUMSTICKS

Preparation Time: 10 minutes
Cooking Time: 5 hours
Servings: 2
Ingredients:

- 10 drumsticks, skin removed
- 1 thick stalk fresh lemongrass
- 4 cloves garlic, minced
- 1 thumb-size piece of ginger
- 1 cup of coconut milk
- 2 tbsp. of Red Boat fish sauce
- 3 tbsp of coconut aminos
- 1 tsp. of five-spice powder
- 1 large onion, sliced
- ¼ cup of fresh scallions, diced
- Kosher salt
- Black pepper

Directions:
1. Start by throwing all the Ingredient into the Crockpot.
2. Cover it and cook for 5 hours on Low Settings.
3. Garnish as desired.
4. Serve warm.

Nutrition:
Calories 372
Total Fat 11.1 g
Saturated Fat 5.8 g
Cholesterol 610 mg
Total Carbs 0.9 g
Polyunsaturated 2.6g
Monounsaturated fats 2.6g
Polyunsaturated fats 1.4g
Net carbs 4.2g

54. GREEN CHILE CHICKEN

Preparation Time: 10 minutes
Cooking Time: 6 hours
Servings: 2
Ingredients:

- 8 chicken thighs, thawed, boneless and skinless
- 1 (4 g) can green chilis
- 2 tsp. of garlic salt
- optional: add in ½ cup of diced onions

Directions:
1. Start by throwing all the Ingredients: into the Crockpot.
2. Cover it and cook for 6 hours on Low Settings.
3. Garnish as desired.
4. Serve warm.

Nutrition:
Calories 248
Total Fat 2.4 g
Saturated Fat 0.1 g
Cholesterol 320 mg
Total Carbs 2.9 g
Polyunsaturated 2.6g
Monounsaturated fats 2.6g
Polyunsaturated fats 1.4g
Net Carbs: 1.2g

55. GARLIC BUTTER CHICKEN WITH CREAM CHEESE SAUCE

Preparation Time: 10 minutes
Cooking Time: 6 hours
Servings: 2
Ingredients:
For the garlic chicken:

- 8 garlic cloves, sliced
- 1.5 tsp. of salt
- 1 stick of butter
- 2 2.5 lbs. of chicken breasts
- Optional 1 onion, sliced

For the cream cheese sauce:

- 8 g of cream cheese
- 1 cup of chicken stock
- salt to taste

Directions:
1. Start by throwing all the Ingredients: for garlic chicken into the Crockpot.
2. Cover it and cook for 6 hours on Low Settings.
3. Now stir cook all the Ingredients: for cream cheese sauce in a saucepan.
4. Once heated, pour this sauce over the cooked chicken.
5. Garnish as desired.
6. Serve warm.

Nutrition:
Calories 301
Total Fat 12.2 g
Saturated Fat 2.4 g
Cholesterol 110 mg
Total Carbs 1.5 g
Polyunsaturated 2.6g
Monounsaturated fats 2.6g
Polyunsaturated fats 1.4g
Net Carbs: 2.3g

56. JERK CHICKEN

Preparation Time: 10 minutes
Cooking Time: 6 hours
Servings: 2
Ingredients:

- 5 drumsticks and 5 wings
- 4 tsp. of salt
- 4 tsp. of paprika
- 1 tsp. of cayenne pepper
- 2 tsp. of onion powder
- 2 tsp. of thyme
- 2 tsp. of white pepper
- 2 tsp. of garlic powder
- 1 tsp. of black pepper

Directions:
1. Start by throwing all the Ingredients: into the Crockpot.
2. Cover it and cook for 6 hours on Low Settings.
3. Garnish as desired.
4. Serve warm.

Nutrition:
Calories 249
Total Fat 11.9 g
Saturated Fat 1.7 g
Cholesterol 78 mg
Total Carbs 1.8 g
Fiber 1.1 g
Sugar 0.3 g
Sodium 79 mg
Potassium 264 mg
Protein 35 g
Net Carbs: 1.8g

57. CHEESE AND PRAWNS

Preparation Time: 10 minutes
Cooking Time: 1 hour 20 minutes
Servings: 2
Ingredients:

- Shallots – 2, finely chopped
- Apple cider vinegar – ¼ cup
- Butter – 2 tbsp.
- Raw prawns – 4 lbs., peeled, rinsed, patted dry
- Almond meal – 2 tsp.
- Swiss cheese – 1 cup, grated
- Garlic – 2 cloves, peeled, thinly sliced
- Hot pepper sauce – ¼ tsp.
- Salt to taste
- Fresh parsley to serve

Directions:
1. Melt butter in a skillet over medium heat. Then add shallots and sauté for a few minutes until translucent.
2. Add prawns and sauté for 2 minutes. Set aside.
3. Grease the inside of the pot with a little butter.
4. Sprinkle garlic over it and add cheese.
5. In a bowl, mix almond meal, apple cider, and hot sauce. Pour the mixture into the Crock-Pot. Stir.
6. Cover and cook on low for 1 hour.
7. Add the prawn shallot mixture and stir.
8. Cover and cook on low for 10 minutes.
9. Stir again and sprinkle parsley over it.
10. Serve.

Nutrition:
Calories: 238
Fat: 13.5g
Carbs: 9g
Protein: 20g
Monounsaturated fats 2.6g
Polyunsaturated 1.6g
Net carbs 4.2g

58. CREAMY SMOKED SALMON SOUP

Preparation Time: 10 minutes
Cooking Time: 3 hours
Servings: 2
Ingredients:

- Smoked salmon – ½ lb., roughly chopped
- Garlic – 3 cloves, crushed
- Small onion – 1, finely chopped
- Leek – 1, finely chopped
- Heavy cream – 1 ½ cups
- Olive oil – 2 tbsp.
- Salt and pepper to taste
- Fish stock – 1 ½ cups

Directions:
1. Add oil into the Crock-Pot.
2. Add fish stock, leek, salmon, garlic, and onion into the pot.
3. Cover with the lid and cook on low for 2 hours.
4. Add the cream and stir. Cook for 1 hour more.
5. Adjust seasoning and serve.

Nutrition:
Calories: 309
Fat: 26.4g
Carbs: 7g
Protein: 12.3g
Monounsaturated fats 2.6g
Polyunsaturated 1.6g
Net carbs 4.2g

59. SALMON CAKE

Preparation Time: 10 minutes
Cooking Time: 4 hours
Servings: 2
Ingredients:

- Eggs – 4, lightly beaten
- Heavy cream – 3 tbsp.
- Baby spinach – 1 cup, roughly chopped
- Smoked salmon strips – 4 ounces, chopped
- A handful of fresh coriander, roughly chopped
- Olive oil – 2 tbsp.
- Salt and pepper to taste

Directions:

1. Drizzle oil into the Crock-Pot.
2. Place the spinach, cream, beaten egg, salmon, salt, and pepper into the pot and mix to combine.
3. Cover with the lid and cook on low for 4 hours.

Nutrition:
Calories: 277
Fat: 20.8g
Carbs: 1.1g
Monounsaturated fats 2.6g
Polyunsaturated 1.6g
Net carbs 4.2g
Protein: 22.5g

60. CHEESY SALMON BITES

Preparation Time: 10 minutes
Cooking Time: 2 hours
Servings: 2
Ingredients:

- Smoked salmon – 4 strips, cut in half lengthways
- Firm cream cheese – ¼ lb., cut into 8 chunks
- Mozzarella cheese – ¼ lb., cut into 8 chunks
- Spring onion – 1, finely chopped
- Lemon – 1, zest
- Olive oil – 2 tbsp.

Directions:
1. Press one piece of mozzarella and one piece of cream cheese together. Sprinkle with a small amount of spring onion.
2. Wrap the cheese bundle in smoked salmon.
3. Repeat the process with the remaining Ingredients.
4. Drizzle oil into the Crock-Pot and place salmon bites in one layer into the pot.
5. Secure the lid and cook on low for 2 hours.
6. Garnish with lemon zest and serve.

Nutrition:
Calories: 195
Fat: 17.1g
Carbs: 3.7g
Protein: 7.9g
Monounsaturated fats 2.6g
Polyunsaturated 1.6g
Net carbs 4.2g

61. COCONUT FISH CURRY

Preparation Time: 10 minutes
Cooking Time: 4 hours
Servings: 2
Ingredients:

- Large white fish fillets – 4, cut into chunks
- Garlic cloves – 4, crushed
- Small onion – 1, finely chopped
- Ground turmeric – 1 tsp.
- Yellow curry paste – 2 tbsp.
- Fish stock – 2 cups
- Full-fat coconut milk – 2 cans
- Lime – 1
- Fresh coriander as needed, roughly chopped
- Olive oil – 2 tbsp.
- Salt and pepper to taste

Directions:
1.   Add olive oil into the Crock-Pot.
2.   Add the coconut milk, stock, fish, curry paste, turmeric, onion, garlic, salt, and pepper to the pot. Stir to combine.
3.   Cover with the lid and cook on high for 4 hours.
4.   Drizzle with lime juice and fresh coriander and serve.

Nutrition:
Calories: 562
Fat: 49.9g
Carbs: 13g
Protein: 20.6g
Monounsaturated fats 2.6g
Polyunsaturated 1.6g
Net carbs 4.2g

62. COCONUT LIME MUSSELS

Preparation Time: 10 minutes
Cooking Time: 2 ½ hours
Servings: 2
Ingredients:

- Fresh mussels – 16
- Garlic – 4 cloves
- Full-fat coconut milk – 1 ½ cups
- Red chili – ½, finely chopped
- Lime – 1, juiced
- Fish stock – ½ cup
- A handful of fresh coriander
- Olive oil – 2 tbsp.
- Salt and pepper to taste

Directions:
1.   Add olive oil into the Crock-Pot.
2.   Add the coconut milk, garlic, chili, fish stock, salt, pepper, and juice of one lime to the pot. Stir to mix.
3.   Cover with the lid and cook on high for 2 hours.
4.   Remove the lid, place mussels into the liquid, and cover with the lid.
5.   Cook until mussels open, about 20 minutes.
6.   Serve the mussels with pot sauce. Garnish with fresh coriander.

Nutrition:
Calories: 342
Fat: 30.2g
Carbs: 11.3g
Protein: 10.9g
Monounsaturated fats 2.6g
Polyunsaturated 1.6g
Net carbs 4.2g

63. CLAM CHOWDER

Preparation Time: 10 minutes
Cooking Time: 2 hours
Servings: 2
Ingredients:

- Chopped celery – ½ cup
- Chopped onion – ½ cup
- Chicken broth – 1 cup
- Whole baby clams with juice – 2 cans
- Heavy whipping cream – 1 cup
- Salt – ½ tsp.
- Ground thyme – ½ tsp.
- Pepper – ½ tsp.

Directions:
1.   Except for the cream, add everything in the Crock-Pot.
2.   Cover and cook on high for 1 hour and 45 minutes.
3.   Then add the cream and cook on high for 15 minutes more.
4.   Serve.

Nutrition:
Calories: 427
Monounsaturated fats 2.6g

Polyunsaturated 1.6g
Net carbs 4.2g
Fat: 33g
Carbs: 5g
Protein: 27g

64. CALAMARI, PRAWN, AND SHRIMP PASTA SAUCE

Preparation Time: 10 minutes
Cooking Time: 3 hours
Servings: 2
Ingredients:
- Calamari – 1 cup
- Prawns – 1 cup
- Shrimp – 1 cup
- Garlic – 6 cloves, crushed
- Tomatoes – 4, chopped
- Dried mixed herbs – 1 tsp.
- Balsamic vinegar - 1 tbsp.
- Olive oil – 2 tbsp.
- Salt and pepper to taste
- Water – ½ cup

Directions:
1. Add oil into the Crock-Pot.
2. Add the tomatoes, garlic, shrimp, prawns, calamari, mixed herbs, balsamic vinegar, water, salt, and pepper. Stir to mix.
3. Cover with the lid and cook on high for 3 hours.
4. Serve with zucchini noodles or veggies.

Nutrition:
Calories: 372
Fat: 14.6g
Monounsaturated fats 2.6g
Polyunsaturated 1.6g
Net carbs 4.2g
Carbs: 8.5g
Protein: 55.1g

65. SESAME PRAWNS

Preparation Time: 10 minutes
Cooking Time: 2 hours
Servings: 2
Ingredients:
- Large prawns – 3 cups
- Garlic – 4 cloves, crushed
- Sesame oil – 1 tbsp.
- Toasted sesame seeds – 2 tbsp.
- Red chili – ½, finely chopped
- Fish stock – ½ cup
- Salt and pepper to taste
- Chopped herbs for serving

Directions:
1. Drizzle the sesame oil into the Crock-Pot.
2. Add the garlic, prawns, sesame seeds, chili, and fish stock to the pot. Mix to coat.
3. Cover with the lid and cook on high for 2 hours.
4. Serve hot with fresh herbs and cauliflower rice.

Nutrition:
Calories: 236
Fat: 7.7g
Carbs: 4.3g
Monounsaturated fats 2.6g
Polyunsaturated 1.6g
Net carbs 4.2g
Protein: 37.4g

66. LEMON-BUTTER FISH

Preparation Time: 10 minutes
Cooking Time: 5 hours
Servings: 2
Ingredients:
- Fresh white fish – 4 fillets
- Butter - 1 ½ ounce, soft but not melted
- Garlic cloves – 2, crushed
- Lemon – 1 (juice and zest)
- A handful of fresh parsley, finely chopped
- Salt and pepper to taste
- Olive oil – 2 tbsp.

Directions:
1. Combine the butter, garlic, zest of one lemon, and chopped parsley to a bowl.
2. Drizzle oil into the Crock-Pot.
3. Season the fish with salt and pepper and place into the pot.
4. Place a dollop of lemon butter onto each fish fillet and gently spread it out.
5. Cover with the lid and cook on low for 5 hours.
6. Serve each fish fillet with a generous spoonful of melted lemon butter from the bottom of the pot. Drizzle with lemon juice and serve.

Nutrition:
Calories: 202
Fat: 13.4g
Monounsaturated fats 2.6g
Polyunsaturated 1.6g
Net carbs 4.2g
Carbs: 1.3g
Protein: 20.3g

67. CHARRED TENDERLOIN WITH LEMON CHIMICHURRI

Preparation Time: 10 minutes
Cooking Time: 50 minutes
Servings: 2
Ingredients:

- Lemon Chimichurri
- lemon, juiced
- ¼ cup chopped mint leaves
- ¼ cup chopped oregano leaves
- cloves garlic, minced
- ¼ cup olive oil
- Salt to taste
- Pork
- 1 (4 lb.) pork tenderloin
- Salt and black pepper to season
- Olive oil for rubbing

Directions:
1. Make the lemon chimichurri to have the flavors incorporate while the pork cooks.
2. In a bowl, mix the mint, oregano, and garlic. Then, add the lemon juice, olive oil, and salt, and combine well. Set the sauce aside at room temperature.
3. Preheat the charcoal grill to 450°F in medium heat creating a direct heat area and indirect heat area. Rub the pork with olive oil, season with salt and pepper. Place the meat over direct heat and sear for 3 minutes on each side, after which, move to the indirect heat area.
4. Close the lid. Cook for 25 minutes on each side, then open, turn the meat, and grill for 20 minutes on the other side. Pull out the pork from the grill and let it sit for 5 minutes before slicing. Spoon lemon chimichurri over the pork and serve with fresh salad.
Nutrition:
388 calories

18g Fat
28g Protein

68. PORK NACHOS

Preparation Time: 10 minutes
Cooking Time: 15 minutes
Servings: 2
Ingredients:

- bag low carb tortilla chips
- cups leftover pulled pork
- 1 red bell pepper, seeded and chopped
- 1 red onion, diced
- cups shredded Monterey Jack cheese

Directions:
1. Preheat oven to 350°F. Arrange the chips in a medium cast-iron pan, scatter pork over, followed by red bell pepper, and onion, and sprinkle with cheese. Place the pan in the oven and cook for 10 minutes until the cheese has melted. Allow cooling for 3 minutes and serve.
Nutrition:
452 calories
25g Fat
22g Protein

69. HERB PORK CHOPS WITH RASPBERRY SAUCE

Preparation Time: 10 minutes
Cooking Time: 17 minutes
Servings: 2
Ingredients:

- 1 tbsp. olive oil + extra for brushing
- lb. pork chops
- Pink salt and black pepper to taste
- cups raspberries
- ¼ cup water
- 1 ½ tbsp. Italian Herb mix
- tbsp. balsamic vinegar
- 2 tsp sugar-free Worcestershire sauce

Directions:
1. Cook oil in a skillet over medium heat, season the pork well and cook for 5 minutes on both sides. Put on serving plates and reserve the pork drippings.
2. Puree the raspberries with a fork in a bowl until jam-like. Pour into a saucepan, add the water, and herb mix. Bring to boil on low heat for 4 minutes. Stir in pork drippings, vinegar, and Worcestershire

sauce. Simmer for 1 minute. Scoop sauce over the pork chops and serve with braised rapini.

Nutrition:

413 calories

32.5g Fat

26.3g Protein

70. GARLICKY PORK WITH BELL PEPPERS

Preparation Time: 10 minutes

Cooking Time: 40 minutes

Servings: 2

Ingredients:

- 3 tbsp. butter
- 4 pork steaks, bone-in
- cup chicken stock
- Salt and black pepper, to taste
- A pinch of lemon pepper
- 2 tbsp. olive oil
- 6 garlic cloves, minced
- 1 tbsp. fresh parsley, chopped
- bell peppers, sliced
- 1 lemon, sliced

Directions:

1. Preheat a pan with 2 tablespoons oil and 2 tablespoons butter over medium heat. Add in the pork steaks, season with black pepper and salt, and cook until browned; remove to a plate. In the same pan, warm the rest of the oil and butter, add garlic and bell peppers and cook for 4 minutes.

2. Pour the chicken stock, lemon slices, salt, lemon pepper, and black pepper, and cook everything for 5 minutes. Place the pork steaks back to the pan and cook for 10 minutes. Split the sauce and steaks among plates and sprinkle with parsley to serve.

Nutrition:

456 calories,

25g Fat

40g Protein

71. PORK BURGERS WITH CARAMELIZED ONION RINGS

Preparation Time: 10 minutes

Cooking Time: 20 minutes

Servings: 2

Ingredients:

- 2 lb. ground pork

- Pink salt and chili pepper to taste
- 3 tbsp. olive oil
- 1 tbsp. butter
- 1 white onion, sliced into rings
- 1 tbsp. balsamic vinegar
- drops liquid stevia
- 6 low carb burger buns, halved
- firm tomatoes, sliced into rings

Directions:

1. Combine the pork, salt and chili pepper in a bowl and mold out 6 patties.

2. Heat the olive oil in a skillet over medium heat and fry the patties for 5 minutes on each side. Remove onto a plate and sit for 3 minutes.

3. Melt butter in a skillet over medium heat, sauté onions for 2 minutes, and stir in the balsamic vinegar and liquid stevia. Cook for 30 seconds stirring once or twice until caramelized. In each bun, place a patty, top with some onion rings and 2 tomato rings. Serve the burgers with cheddar cheese dip.

Nutrition:

445 calories

32g Fat

26g Protein

72. LEMON PORK CHOPS WITH BUTTERED BRUSSELS SPROUTS

Preparation Time: 10 minutes

Cooking Time: 27 minutes

Servings: 2

Ingredients:

- 3 tbsp. lemon juice
- 3 cloves garlic, pureed
- 1 tbsp. olive oil
- 6 pork loin chops
- 1 tbsp. butter
- 1 lb. brussels sprouts, trimmed and halved
- 2 tbsp. white wine
- Salt and black pepper to taste

Directions:

1. Preheat broiler to 400°F and mix the lemon juice, garlic, salt, black pepper, and oil in a bowl.

2. Brush the pork with the mixture, place in a baking sheet, and cook for 6 minutes on each side

until browned. Share into 6 plates and make the side dish.

3.   Melt butter in a small wok or pan and cook in Brussels sprouts for 5 minutes until tender. Drizzle with white wine, sprinkle with salt and black pepper and cook for another 5 minutes. Ladle Brussels sprouts to the side of the chops and serve with a hot sauce.

Nutrition:

549 calories

48g Fat

26g Protein

73.   PORK   CHOPS   WITH CRANBERRY SAUCE

Preparation Time: 30 minutes

Cooking Time: 2 hours 10 minutes

Servings: 2

Ingredients:

- 4 pork chops
- tsp garlic powder
- Salt and black pepper, to taste
- 1 tsp fresh basil, chopped
- A drizzle of olive oil
- 1 shallot, chopped
- 1 cup white wine
- 1 bay leaf
- cups vegetable stock
- Fresh parsley, chopped, for serving
- 2 cups cranberries
- ½ tsp fresh rosemary, chopped
- ½ cup swerve
- Juice of 1 lemon
- cup water
- 1 tsp harissa paste

Directions:

1.   In a bowl, combine the pork chops with 2 tsp of basil, salt, garlic powder and black pepper. Preheat a pan with a dash of oil over medium heat, place in the pork and cook until browned; set aside.

2.   Mix in the shallot, and cook for 2 minutes. Place in the bay leaf and wine, and cook for 4 minutes. Pour in juice from ½ lemon, and vegetable stock, and simmer for 5 minutes. Return the pork, and cook for 10 minutes. Cover the pan, and place in the oven to bake at 350°F for 2 hours.

3.   Set a pan over medium heat, add cranberries, rosemary, harissa paste, water, 1 tsp basil, swerve, and juice from ½ lemon, simmer for 15 minutes. Remove the pork chops from the oven, remove and discard the bay leaf. Split among plates, spread over with the cranberry sauce, sprinkle with parsley to serve.

Nutrition:

450 calories,

34g Fat

26g Protein

74.   BALSAMIC   GRILLED   PORK CHOPS

Preparation Time: 20 minutes

Cooking Time: 2 hours 20 minutes

Servings: 2

Ingredients:

- 6 pork loin chops, boneless
- 2 tbsp. erythritol
- ¼ cup balsamic vinegar
- 3 cloves garlic, minced
- ¼ cup olive oil
- 1/3 tsp salt
- Black pepper to taste

Directions:

1.   Put the pork in a plastic bag. In a bowl, mix the erythritol, balsamic vinegar, garlic, olive oil, salt, pepper, and pour the sauce over the pork. Seal the bag, shake it, and place in the refrigerator.

2.   Marinate the pork for 2 hours. Prepare the grill to medium heat, remove the pork when ready, and grill covered for 10 minutes on each side. Take it out and let sit for 4 minutes, and serve with parsnip sauté.

Nutrition:

418 calories

26.8g Fat

38.1g Protein

75.   PORK IN WHITE WINE

Preparation Time: 10 minutes

Cooking Time: 1 hour 15 minutes

Servings: 2

Ingredients:

- 2 tbsp. olive oil
- 2 pounds pork stew meat, cubed
- Salt and black pepper, to taste

- 2 tbsp. butter
- 4 garlic cloves, minced
- ¾ cup vegetable stock
- ½ cup white wine
- 3 carrots, chopped
- cabbage head, shredded
- ½ cup scallions, chopped
- 1 cup heavy cream

Directions:

1. Position a pan over medium heat and warm butter and oil. Sear the pork until brown. Add garlic, scallions and carrots; sauté for 5 minutes.

2. Pour in the cabbage, stock and wine, and bring to a boil. Reduce the heat and cook for 1 hour covered. Add in heavy cream as you stir for 1 minute, adjust seasonings and serve.

Nutrition:
514 calories
32.5g Fat
43g Protein

76. STUFFED PORK WITH RED CABBAGE SALAD

Preparation Time: 10 minutes
Cooking Time: 40 minutes
Servings: 2
Ingredients:

- Zest and juice from 2 limes
- 2 garlic cloves, minced
- ¾ cup olive oil
- cup fresh cilantro, chopped
- 1 cup fresh mint, chopped
- 1 tsp dried oregano
- Salt and black pepper, to taste
- 1 tsp cumin
- pork loin steaks
- 2 pickles, chopped
- ham slices
- Swiss cheese slices
- 2 tbsp. mustard

For the Salad

- head red cabbage, shredded
- 1 tbsp. vinegar
- 1 tbsp. olive oil
- Salt to taste

Directions:

1. In a food processor, blitz the lime zest, oil, oregano, black pepper, cumin, cilantro, lime juice, garlic, mint, and salt. Rub the steaks with the mixture and toss well to coat; set aside for some hours in the fridge.

2. Arrange the steaks on a working surface, split the pickles, mustard, cheese, and ham on them, roll, and secure with toothpicks. Preheat a pan over medium heat, mix in the pork rolls, cook each side for 2 minutes and remove to a baking sheet. Cook for 25 minutes at 350°Farenheit in the oven. Prepare the red cabbage salad by mixing all salad ingredients and serve with the meat.

Nutrition:
413 calories
37g Fat
26g Protein

77. BAKED PORK MEATBALLS IN PASTA SAUCE

Preparation Time: 10 minutes
Cooking Time: 45 minutes
Servings: 2
Ingredients:

- 2 lb. ground pork
- 1 tbsp. olive oil
- 1 cup pork rinds, crushed
- cloves garlic, minced
- ½ cup coconut milk
- eggs, beaten
- ½ cup grated Parmesan cheese
- ½ cup grated asiago cheese
- Salt and black pepper to taste
- ¼ cup chopped parsley
- 2 jars sugar-free marinara sauce
- ½ tsp Italian seasoning
- 1 cup Italian blend kinds of cheeses
- Chopped basil to garnish

Directions:

1. Ready the oven to 400°F, wrap the cast iron pan with foil and oil it with cooking spray. Set aside.

2. Combine the coconut milk and pork rinds in a bowl. Mix in the ground pork, garlic, Asiago cheese, Parmesan cheese, eggs, salt, and pepper, just until combined. Form balls of the mixture and place them

in the prepared pan. Bake in the oven for 20 minutes at a reduced temperature of 370°F.

3.   Transfer the meatballs to a plate. Fill half of the marinara sauce in the baking pan. Place the meatballs back in the pan and pour the remaining marinara sauce all over them. Sprinkle with the Italian blend cheeses, drizzle with the olive oil, and then sprinkle with Italian seasoning.

4.   Cover the pan with foil and put it back in the oven to bake for 10 minutes. After, remove the foil, and cook for 5 minutes. Once ready, take out the pan and garnish with basil. Serve on a bed of squash spaghetti.

Nutrition:
590 calories
46.8g Fat
46.2g Protein

78.   GRILLED PORK LOIN CHOPS WITH BARBECUE SAUCE

Preparation Time: 10 minutes
Cooking Time: 2 hours 15 minutes
Servings: 2
Ingredients:

*   4 (6 oz.) thick-cut pork loin chops, boneless
*   ½ cup sugar-free BBQ sauce
*   tsp black pepper
*   1 tbsp. erythritol
*   ½ tsp ginger powder
*   tsp sweet paprika

Directions:

1.   In a bowl, mix pepper, erythritol, ginger powder, and sweet paprika, and rub the pork on all sides with the mixture. Cover the pork chops with plastic wraps and place it in the fridge to marinate for 2 hours.

2.   Preheat the grill to 450°F. Unwrap the meat, place on the grill grate, and cook for 2 minutes per side. Reduce the heat and brush the BBQ sauce on the meat, cover and grill them for 5 minutes.

3.   Open the lid, turn the meat and brush again with barbecue sauce. Continue cooking covered for 5 minutes. Transfer the meat in a platter and serve with mixed steamed vegetables.

Nutrition:
363 calories
26.6g Fat
34.1g Protein

79.   PORK SAUSAGE BAKE

Preparation Time: 10 minutes
Cooking Time: 50 minutes
Servings: 2
Ingredients:

*   12 pork sausages
*   5 large tomatoes, cut in rings
*   red bell pepper, seeded and sliced
*   yellow bell pepper, seeded and sliced
*   1 green bell pepper, seeded and sliced
*   1 sprig thyme, chopped
*   1 sprig rosemary, chopped
*   4 cloves garlic, minced
*   bay leaves
*   1 tbsp. olive oil
*   1 tbsp. balsamic vinegar

Directions:

1.   Preheat the oven to 350°F.

2.   In the cast iron pan, add the tomatoes, bell peppers, thyme, rosemary, garlic, bay leaves, olive oil, and balsamic vinegar. Toss everything and arrange the sausages on top of the veggies.

3.   Put the pan in the oven and bake for 20 minutes. After, remove the pan shake it a bit and turn the sausages over with a spoon. Continue cooking for 25 minutes. Serve with the veggie and cooking sauce with cauli rice.

Nutrition:
465 calories
41.6g Fat
15.1g Protein

80.   PORK   PIE   WITH CAULIFLOWER

Preparation Time: 10 minutes
Cooking Time: 1 hour and 30 minutes
Servings: 2
Ingredients:
Crust:

*   egg
*   ¼ cup butter
*   cups almond flour
*   ¼ tsp xanthan gum
*   ¼ cup shredded mozzarella
*   A pinch of salt

Filling:

- 2 pounds ground pork
- ½ cup water
- 1/3 cup pureed onion
- ¾ tsp allspice
- cup cooked and mashed cauliflower
- 1 tbsp. ground sage
- 1 tbsp. butter

Directions:

1. Preheat your oven to 350°F.
2. Whisk together all crust ingredients in a bowl. Make two balls out of the mixture and refrigerate for 10 minutes. Combine the water, meat, and salt, in a pot over medium heat. Cook for about 15 minutes, place the meat along with the other ingredients in a bowl. Mix with your hands to combine.
3. Roll out the pie crusts and place one at the bottom of a greased pie pan. Spread the filling over the crust. Top with the other coat. Cook in the oven for 49 minutes then serve.

Nutrition:

485 calories
41g Fat
29g Protein

81. PORK OSSO BUCCO

Preparation Time: 20 minutes
Cooking Time: 1 hour 35 minutes
Servings: 2
Ingredients:

- 4 tbsp. butter, softened
- 6 (16 oz.) pork shanks
- 2 tbsp. olive oil
- 3 cloves garlic, minced
- cup diced tomatoes
- Salt and black pepper to taste
- ½ cup chopped onions
- ½ cup chopped celery
- ½ cup chopped carrots
- 2 cups Cabernet Sauvignon
- 5 cups vegetable broth
- ½ cup chopped parsley + extra to garnish
- 2 tsp lemon zest

Directions:

1. Melt the butter in a huge saucepan over medium heat. Season the pork with salt and black pepper and brown it for 12 minutes; remove to a plate.
2. In the same pan, sauté 2 cloves of garlic and onions in the oil, for 3 minutes; return the pork shanks. Stir in the Cabernet, carrots, celery, tomatoes, and vegetable broth; season with salt and pepper. Close and simmer on low heat for 1 ½ hours basting the pork every 15 minutes with the sauce.
3. In a bowl, mix the remaining garlic, parsley, and lemon zest to make a gremolata, and stir the mixture into the sauce when it is ready. Turn the heat off and dish the Osso Bucco. Garnish with parsley and serve with creamy turnip mash.

Nutrition:

590 calories
40g Fat
34g Protein

82. MACKEREL PACKETS

Preparation Time: 10 minutes
Cooking Time: 25 minutes
Servings: 2
Ingredients:

- 3 large Whole Mackerel, cut into 2 pieces
- 6 medium Tomatoes, quartered
- large Brown Onion, sliced thinly
- 1 Orange Bell pepper, seeded and chopped
- Salt and black pepper to taste
- ½ tbsp. Pernod
- cloves Garlic, minced
- 2 Lemons, halved
- 1 ½ cups Water

Directions:

1. Cut out 6 pieces of parchment paper a little longer and wider than a piece of fish with kitchen scissors. Then, cut out 6 pieces of foil slightly longer than the parchment papers.
2. Lay the foil wraps on a flat surface and place each parchment paper on each aluminum foil. In a bowl, add the tomatoes, onions, garlic, bell pepper, Pernod, salt, and pepper. Use a spoon to mix them.
3. Place each fish piece on the layer of parchment and foil wraps. Spoon the tomato mixture on each fish. Then, wrap the fish and place the fish packets in the refrigerator to marinate for 2 hours. After 2 hours, remove the fish onto a flat surface.

4.   Open the Instant Pot, pour the water into and fit the trivet at the bottom of the pot. Put the packets on the trivet. Close the lid, secure the pressure valve, and select Steam on High pressure for 5 minutes. Once ready, do a quick pressure release. Remove the trivet with the fish packets onto a flat surface.

5.   Carefully open the foil and use a spoon to dish the soup with vegetables and sauce onto serving plates. Serve with a side of roasted daikon radish and the lemon wedges.

Nutrition:

95 Calories

10.9g Protein

5.3g Fat

83.   FENNEL ALASKAN COD WITH TURNIPS

Preparation Time: 10 minutes

Cooking Time: 20 minutes

Servings: 2

Ingredients:

- 2 (18 oz.) Alaskan Cod, cut into 4 pieces each
- 4 tbsp. Olive oil
- 2 cloves Garlic, minced
- 2 small Onions, chopped
- ½ cup Olive Brine
- 2 cups Chicken Broth
- Salt and black pepper to taste
- ½ cup sugar-free Tomato Puree
- head Fennel, quartered
- Turnips, peeled and quartered
- 1 cup Green Olives, pitted and crushed
- 1/2 cup Basil Leaves
- Lemon Slices to garnish

Directions:

1.   Turn on the Instant Pot, open the pot, and select Sauté mode. Pour the olive oil, once heated add the garlic and onion. Stir fry them until the onion has softened. Pour the chicken broth in and tomato puree. Let simmer for about 3 minutes.

2.   Add the fennel, olives, turnips, salt, and pepper. Close the lid, secure the pressure valve, and select Steam mode on Low pressure for 8 minutes. Once ready, do a quick pressure release. Transfer the vegetables onto a plate with a slotted spoon.

3.   Adjust broth's taste with salt and pepper and add the cod pieces. Close the lid again, secure the pressure valve, and select Steam mode on Low pressure for 3 minutes. Once ready, do a quick pressure release.

4.   Remove the cod into soup plates, top with the veggies and basil leaves, and spoon the broth over them. Serve with a side of low carb crusted bread.

Nutrition:

64 Calories

14.8g Protein

4.3g Fat

84.   SWEET & SPICY MAHI-MAHI

Preparation Time: 10 minutes

Cooking Time: 10 minutes

Servings: 2

Ingredients:

- 4 Mahi-Mahi Fillets, fresh
- 4 cloves Garlic, minced
- ¼ -inch Ginger, grated
- Salt and black pepper to taste
- 1 tbsp. Chili Powder
- 1 tbsp. Sriracha Sauce
- 1 ½ tbsp. Monk Fruit Syrup
- 1 Lime, juiced

Directions:

1.   Place the mahi-mahi on a plate and season with salt and pepper on both sides. In a bowl, add the garlic, ginger, chili powder, sriracha sauce, monk fruit syrup, and lime juice. Use a spoon to mix it. With a brush, apply the hot sauce mixture on the fillet.

2.   Fill 1 cup of water into the pot and fit in a trivet. Put the fillets on the trivet. Seal the lid and select Steam on High for 5 minutes. Once ready, do a quick pressure release. Use tongs to pull out the mahi-mahi onto serving plates. Serve with steamed or braised asparagus.

Nutrition:

130 Calories

34g Protein

2g Fat

85. SALMON IN SPICY LIME SAUCE

Preparation Time: 10 minutes
Cooking Time: 20 minutes
Servings: 2
Ingredients:
Salmon:

- 3 Salmon Fillets, cut into 2
- cup Water
- Salt and black pepper to taste
- Spicy Lime Sauce:
- Jalapenos, seeded and diced
- Limes, juices
- cloves Garlic, minced
- 1 tbsp. Monk Fruit Syrup
- 2 tbsp. Olive oil
- 2 tbsp. Hot Water, (make a quick one in the microwave)
- 2 sprigs Parsley, minced
- 1 tsp Paprika
- 1 tsp Cumin

Directions:
1.   Incorporate all sauce ingredients in a bowl, mix well and set aside. Pour water in the pot and fit a steamer basket in. Arrange salmon in the basket and sprinkle with pepper and salt; don't mix. Seal the lid, select Manual and cook on High Pressure mode for 5 minutes. Once ready, quickly release the pressure. Place the salmon to a plate and drizzle the spicy sauce over.
Nutrition:
415 Calories
29g Protein
25g Fat

86. FISH SOUL-SATISFYING SOUP

Preparation Time: 10 minutes
Cooking Time: 35 minutes
Servings: 2
Ingredients:

- 1 tbsp. saffron
- 1 tbsp. Garlic paste
- Salt and black pepper to taste
- Fish fillets, cut into pieces
- 1 cup Cream
- 1 pinch Chili powder
- 1 cup Almond Milk
- 1 tbsp. Olive oil

Directions:
1.   Heat oil in on Sauté mode and cook garlic and onion for 2 minutes. Stir in the fish and cook until golden brown, for 5 minutes. Season with salt and chili powder. Shred the fish with a fork.
2.   Add in the cream and milk, mix well. Cook for 10 minutes on Manual mode on High pressure. When ready, do a quick pressure release. Top with chili powder and saffron to serve.
Nutrition:
587 Calories
29.1g Protein
51.4g Fat

CHAPTER 7. DINNER

87. CHICKEN AVOCADO SALAD

Preparation Time: 7 minutes
Cooking Time: 10 minutes
Servings: 2
Ingredients:

• 1 cup roasted chicken, shredded (Lunch Recipes: Roasted Lemon Chicken Sandwich)
• 1 bacon strip, cooked and chopped
• 1/2 medium avocado, chopped
• ¼ cup cheddar cheese, grated
• 1 hard-boiled egg, chopped
• 1 cup romaine lettuce, chopped
• 1 tbsp. olive oil
• 1 tbsp. apple cider vinegar
• Salt and pepper to taste

Directions:
1. Create the dressing by mixing apple cider vinegar, oil, salt and pepper.
2. Combine all the other ingredients in a mixing bowl.
3. Drizzle with the dressing and toss.
4. Can be refrigerated for up to 3 days.

Nutrition:
Calories: 220 kcal
Carbs: 2.8 g
Fat: 16.7 g
Protein: 14.8 g.

88. CHICKEN BROCCOLI DINNER

Preparation Time: 10 minutes
Cooking Time: 5 minutes
Servings: 1
Ingredients:

• 1 roasted chicken leg (Lunch Recipes: Roasted Lemon Chicken Sandwich)
• ½ cup broccoli florets
• ½ tbsp. unsalted butter, softened
• 2 garlic cloves, minced
• Salt and pepper to taste

Directions:
1. Boil the broccoli in lightly salted water for 5 minutes. Drain the water from the pot and keep the broccoli in the pot. Keep the lid on to keep the broccoli warm.
2. Mix all the butter, garlic, salt and pepper in a small bowl to create garlic butter.
3. Place the chicken, broccoli and garlic butter.

Nutrition:
Calories: 257 kcal
Carbs: 5.1 g
Fat: 14 g
Protein: 27.4 g.

89. EASY MEATBALLS

Preparation Time: 10 minutes
Cooking Time: 20 minutes
Servings: 2
Ingredients:

• 1 lb. ground beef
• 1 egg, beaten
• Salt and pepper to taste
• 1 tsp. garlic powder
• 1 tsp. onion powder
• 2 tbsp. butter
• ¼ cup mayonnaise
• ¼ cup pickled jalapeños
• 1 cup cheddar cheese, grated

Directions:
1. Combine the cheese, mayonnaise, pickled jalapenos, salt, pepper, garlic powder and onion powder in a large mixing bowl.
2. Add the beef and egg and combine using clean hands.
3. Form large meatballs. Makes about 12.
4. Fry the meatballs in the butter over medium heat for about 4 minutes on each side or until golden brown.
5. Serve warm with a keto-friendly side.
6. The meatball mixture can also be used to make a meatloaf. Just preheat your oven to 400 degrees F, press the mixture into a loaf pan and bake for about 30 minutes or until the top is golden brown.
7. Can be refrigerated for up to 5 days or frozen for up to 3 months.

Nutrition:
Calories: 454 kcal
Carbs: 5 g
Fat: 28.2 g
Protein: 43.2 g.

90. CHICKEN CASSEROLE

Preparation Time: 10 minutes
Cooking Time: 40 minutes
Servings: 2
Ingredients:

- 1 lb. boneless chicken breasts, cut into 1" cubes
- 2 tbsp. butter
- 4 tbsp. green pesto
- 1 cup heavy whipping cream
- ¼ cup green bell peppers, diced
- 1 cup feta cheese, diced
- 1 garlic clove, minced
- Salt and pepper to taste

Directions:
1. Preheat your oven to 400 degrees F.
2. Season the chicken with salt and pepper then batch fry in the butter until golden brown.
3. Place the fried chicken pieces in a baking dish. Add the feta cheese, garlic and bell peppers.
4. Combine the pesto and heavy cream in a bowl. Pour on top of the chicken mixture and spread with a spatula.
5. Bake for 30 minutes or until the casserole is light brown around the edges.
6. Serve warm.
7. Can be refrigerated for up to 5 days and frozen for 2 weeks.

Nutrition:
Calories: 294 kcal
Carbs: 1.7 g
Fat: 22.7 g
Protein: 20.1 g.

91. LEMON BAKED SALMON

Preparation Time: 10 minutes
Cooking Time: 30 minutes
Servings: 2
Ingredients:

- 1 lb. salmon
- 1 tbsp. olive oil
- Salt and pepper to taste
- 1 tbsp. butter
- 1 lemon, thinly sliced
- 1 tbsp. lemon juice

Directions:
1. Preheat your oven to 400 degrees F.
2. Grease a baking dish with the olive oil and place the salmon skin-side down.
3. Season the salmon with salt and pepper then top with the lemon slices.

4. Slice half the butter and place over the salmon.
5. Bake for 20minutes or until the salmon flakes easily.
6. Melt the remaining butter in a saucepan. When it starts to bubble, remove from heat and allow to cool before adding the lemon juice.
7. Drizzle the lemon butter over the salmon and Serve warm.

Nutrition:
Calories: 211 kcal
Carbs: 1.5 g
Fat: 13.5 g
Protein: 22.2 g.

92. CAULIFLOWER MASH

Preparation Time: 10 minutes
Cooking Time: 5 minutes
Servings: 2
Ingredients:

- 4 cups cauliflower florets, chopped
- 1 cup grated parmesan cheese
- 6 tbsp. butter
- ½ lemon, juice and zest
- Salt and pepper to taste

Directions:
1. Boil the cauliflower in lightly salted water over high heat for 5 minutes or until the florets are tender but still firm.
2. Strain the cauliflower in a colander and add the cauliflower to a food processor
3. Add the remaining ingredients and pulse the mixture to a smooth and creamy consistency
4. Serve with protein like salmon, chicken or meatballs.
5. Can be refrigerated for up to 3 days.

Nutrition:
Calories: 101 kcal
Carbs: 3.1 g
Fat: 9.5 g
Protein: 2.2 g.

93. ROASTED CHICKEN SOUP

Preparation Time: 10 minutes
Cooking Time: 25 minutes
Servings: 2
Ingredients:

- 4 cups roasted chicken, shredded (Lunch Recipes: Roasted Lemon Chicken Sandwich)

- 2 tbsp. butter
- 2 celery stalks, chopped
- 1 cup mushrooms, sliced
- 4 cups green cabbage, sliced into strips
- 2 garlic cloves, minced
- 6 cups chicken broth
- 1 carrot, sliced
- Salt and pepper to taste
- 1 tbsp. garlic powder
- 1 tbsp. onion powder

Directions:
1. Sauté the celery, mushrooms and garlic in the butter in a pot over medium heat for 4 minutes.
2. Add broth, carrots, garlic powder, onion powder, salt, and pepper.
3. Simmer for 10 minutes or until the vegetables are tender.
4. Add the chicken and cabbage and simmer for another 10 minutes or until the cabbage is tender.
5. Serve warm.
6. Can be refrigerated for up to 3 days or frozen for up to 1 month.

Nutrition:
Calories: 279 kcal
Carbs: 7.5 g
Fat: 12.3 g
Protein: 33.4 g.

94. BAKED SALMON

Preparation Time: 10 minutes
Cooking Time: 10 minutes
Servings: 2
Ingredients:
- Cooking spray
- 3 cloves garlic, minced
- ¼ cup butter
- 1 tsp. lemon zest
- 2 tsp. lemon juice
- 4 salmon fillets
- Salt and pepper to taste
- 2 tbsp. parsley, chopped

Directions:
1. Preheat your oven to 425°F.
2. Grease the pan with cooking spray.
3. In a bowl, mix the garlic, butter, and lemon zest and lemon juice.

4. Sprinkle salt and pepper on salmon fillets.
5. Drizzle with the lemon butter sauce.
6. Bake in the oven for 12 minutes.
7. Garnish with parsley before serving.

Nutrition:
Calories 345
Total Fat 22.7g
Saturated Fat 8.9g
Cholesterol 109mg
Sodium 163mg
Total Carbohydrate 1.2g
Dietary Fiber 0.2g
Total Sugars 0.2g
Protein 34.9g
Potassium 718mg

95. TUNA PATTIES

Preparation Time: 10 minutes
Cooking Time: 10 minutes
Servings: 2
Ingredients:
- 20 oz. canned tuna flakes
- ¼ cup almond flour
- 1 egg, beaten
- 2 tbsp. fresh dill, chopped
- 2 stalks green onion, chopped
- Salt and pepper to taste
- 1 tbsp. lemon zest
- ¼ cup mayonnaise
- 1 tbsp. lemon juice
- 2 tbsp. avocado oil

Directions:
1. Combine all the ingredients except avocado oil, lemon juice and avocado oil in a large bowl.
2. Form 8 patties from the mixture.
3. In a pan over medium heat, add the oil.
4. Once the oil starts to sizzle, cook the tuna patties for 3 to 4 minutes per side.
5. Drain each patty on a paper towel.
6. Spread mayo on top and drizzle with lemon juice before serving.

Nutrition:
Calories 101
Total Fat 4.9g
Saturated Fat 1.2g
Cholesterol 47mg
Sodium 243mg

Total Carbohydrate 3.1g
Dietary Fiber 0.5g
Total Sugars 0.7g
Protein 12.3g
Potassium 60mg

96.   GRILLED MAHI WITH LEMON BUTTER SAUCE

Preparation Time: 20 minutes
Cooking Time: 10 minutes
Servings: 2
Ingredients:
- 6 Mahi fillets
- Salt and pepper to taste
- 2 tbsp. olive oil
- 6 tbsp. butter
- ¼ onion, minced
- ½ teaspoon garlic, minced
- ¼ cup chicken stock
- 1 tablespoon lemon juice

Directions:
1. Preheat your grill to medium heat.
2. Season fish fillets with salt and pepper.
3. Coat both sides with olive oil.
4. Grill for 3 to 4 minutes per side.
5. Place fish on a serving platter.
6. In a pan over medium heat, add the butter and let it melt.
7. Add the onion and sauté for 2 minutes.
8. Add the garlic and cook for 30 seconds.
9. Pour in the chicken stock.
10. Simmer until the stock has been reduced to half.
11. Add the lemon juice.
12. Pour the sauce over the grilled fish fillets.

Nutrition:
Calories 234
Total Fat 17.2g
Saturated Fat 8.3g
Cholesterol 117mg
Sodium 242mg
Total Carbohydrate 0.6g
Dietary Fiber 0.1g
Total Sugars 0.3g
Protein 19.1g
Potassium 385mg

97.   KETO BUFFALO DRUMSTICKS AND CHILI AIOLI

Preparation Time: 12 minutes
Cooking Time: 40 minutes
Servings: 2
Ingredients:
- 2 lbs. chicken drumsticks or chicken wings
- 2 tbsp. olive oil or coconut oil
- 2 tbsp. white wine vinegar
- 1 tbsp. tomato paste
- 1 tsp. salt
- 1 tsp. paprika powder
- 1 tbsp. Tabasco
- Butter or olive oil, for greasing the baking dish

Chili aioli:
- 2/3 cup mayonnaise
- 1 tbsp. smoked paprika powder or smoked chili powder
- 1 garlic clove, minced

Directions:
1. Preheat the oven to 450°F (220°C).
2. Put the drumsticks in a plastic bag.
3. Mix the ingredients for the marinade and pour into the plastic bag. Shake the bag and let marinate for 10 minutes.
4. Coat a baking dish with oil. Place the drumsticks in the baking bowl and let bake for 30–40 minutes or until they are done and have turned a beautiful color.
5. Mix together mayonnaise, garlic, and chili.

Nutrition:
Calories: 409
Protein: 22 Grams
Fat: 10 Grams
Net Carbs: 6 Gram

98.   KETO FISH CASSEROLE

Preparation Time: 10 minutes
Cooking Time: 20 minutes
Servings: 2
Ingredients:
- 2 tbsp. olive oil
- 15 oz. broccoli
- 6 scallions
- 2 tbsp. small capers

- 1/6 oz. butter, for greasing the casserole dish
- 25 oz. white fish, in serving-sized pieces
- 1¼ cups heavy whipping cream
- 1 tbsp. Dijon mustard
- 1 tsp. salt
- ¼ tsp. ground black pepper
- 1 tbsp. dried parsley
- 3 oz. butter

Directions:
1. Preheat the oven to 400°F.
2. Divide the broccoli into smaller floret heads and include the stems. Peel it with a sharp knife or a potato peeler if the stem is rough or leafy.
3. Fry the broccoli florets in oil on a medium-high heat for about 5 minutes, until they are golden and soft. Season with salt and pepper to taste.
4. Add finely chopped scallions and the capers. Fry this for another 1 to 2 minutes and place the vegetables in a baking dish that has been greased.
5. Place the fish tightly in amongst the vegetables.
6. Mix the parsley, whipping cream and mustard together. Pour this over the fish and vegetables. Top it with slices of butter.
7. Bake the fish until it is cooked through, and it flakes easily with a fork. Serve as is, or with a tasty green salad.

Nutrition:
Calories: 314
Protein: 20 Grams
Fat: 8 Grams
Net Carbs: 5 Gram

99. SLOW COOKER KETO PORK ROAST

Preparation Time: 35 minutes
Cooking Time: 8 hours 20 minutes
Servings: 2
Ingredients:
- 30 oz. pork shoulder or pork roast
- ½ tbsp. salt
- 1 bay leaf
- 5 black pep
- per corns
- 2½ cups water
- 2 tsp. dried thyme or dried rosemary
- 2 garlic cloves
- 1½ oz. fresh ginger
- 1 tbsp. olive oil or coconut oil
- 1 tbsp. paprika powder
- ½ tsp. ground black pepper

Creamy gravy:
- 1½ cups heavy whipping cream
- Juices from the roast

Directions:
1. Preheat the oven to a low heat of 200°F.
2. Season the meat with salt and place it into a deep baking dish.
3. Add water. Add a bay leaf, peppercorns, and thyme for more seasoning. Place the baking bowl in the oven for 7 to 8 hours and cover it with aluminum foil.
4. If you are using a slow cooker for this, do the same process as in step 2, only add 1 cup of water. Cook it for 8 hours on low or for 4 hours on high setting.
5. Take the meat out of the baking dish, and reserve the pan juices in a separate pan to make gravy.
6. Turn the oven up to 450°F.
7. Finely chop or press the garlic and ginger into a small bowl. Add the oil, herbs, and pepper and stir well to combine together.
8. Rub the meat with the garlic and herb mixture.
9. Return the meat back to the baking dish, and roast it for about 10 to 15 minutes or until it looks golden-brown.
10. Cut the meat into thin slices to serve it with the creamy gravy and a fibrous vegetable side dish

Gravy:
1. Strain the reserved pan juices to get rid of any solid pieces from the liquid. Boil and reduce the pan juices to about half the original volume, this should be about 1 cup.
2. Pour the reduction into a pot with the whipping cream. Bring this to a boil. Reduce the heat and let it simmer to your desired consistency for a creamy gravy.

Nutrition:
Calories: 432
Protein: 15 Grams
Fat: 29 Grams
Net Carbs: 13 Gram

100. FRIED EGGS WITH KALE AND PORK

Preparation Time: 15 minutes
Cooking Time: 20 minutes
Servings: 2
Ingredients:

- ½ lb. kale
- 3 oz. butter
- 6 oz. smoked pork belly or bacon
- ¼ cup frozen cranberries
- 1 oz. pecans or walnuts
- 4 eggs
- Salt and pepper

Directions:
1.   Cut and chop the kale into large squares. You can use pre-washed baby kale as a shortcut if you want. Melt two-thirds of the butter in a frying pan, and fry the kale on high heat until it is slightly browned around its edges.
2.   Remove the kale from the frying pan and put it aside. Sear the pork belly in the same frying pan until it is crispy.
3.   Turn the heat down. Put the sautéed kale back into the pan and add the cranberries and nuts. Stir this mixture until it is warmed through. Put it into a bowl on the side.
4.   Turn up the heat once more, and fry the eggs in the remaining amount of the butter. Add salt and pepper to taste. Serve the eggs and greens immediately.
Nutrition:
Calories: 180
Protein: 23 Grams
Fat: 30 Grams
Net Carbs: 13 Gram

101. CAULIFLOWER SOUP WITH PANCETTA

Preparation Time: 15 minutes
Cooking Time: 35 minutes
Servings: 2
Ingredients:

- 4 cups chicken broth or vegetable stock
- 15 oz. cauliflower
- 7 oz. cream cheese
- 1 tbsp. Dijon mustard
- 4 oz. butter
- Salt and pepper
- 7 oz. pancetta or bacon, diced
- 1 tbsp. butter, for frying
- 1 tsp. paprika powder or smoked chili powder
- 3 oz. pecans

Directions:
1.   Trim the cauliflower and cut it into smaller floret heads. The smaller the florets are, the quicker the soup will be ready.
2.   Put aside a handful of the fresh cauliflower and chop into small 1/4 inch bits.
3.   Sauté the finely chopped cauliflower and pancetta in butter until it is crispy. Add some nuts and the paprika powder at the end. Set aside the mixture for serving.
4.   Boil the cauliflower until they are soft. Add the cream cheese, mustard, and butter.
5.   Stir the soup well, using an immersion blender, to get to the desired consistency. The creamier the soup will become the longer you blend. Salt and pepper the soup to taste.
6.   Serve soup in bowls, and top it with the fried pancetta mixture.
Nutrition:
Calories: 112
Protein: 10 Grams
Fat: 22 Grams
Net Carbs: 21 Gram

102. BUTTER MAYONNAISE

Preparation Time: 20 minutes
Cooking Time: 25 minutes
Servings: 2
Ingredients:

- 51/3 oz. butter
- 1 egg yolk
- 1 tbsp. Dijon mustard
- 1 tsp lemon juice
- ¼ tsp salt
- 1 pinch ground black pepper

Directions:
1.   Melt the butter in a small saucepan. Pour it into a small pitcher or a jug with a spout and let the butter cool.

2. Mix together egg yolks and mustard in a small-sized bowl. Pour the butter in a thin stream while beating it with a hand mixer. Leave the sediment that settles at the bottom.

3. Keep beating the mixture until the mayonnaise turns thick and creamy. Add some lemon juice. Season it with salt and black pepper. Serve this immediately.

Nutrition:

Calories: 428

Protein: 45 Grams

Fat: 4 Grams

Net Carbs: 14 Gram

103. MEATLOAF WRAPPED IN BACON

Preparation Time: 10 minutes

Cooking Time: 15 minutes

Servings: 2

Ingredients:

- 2 tbsp. butter
- 1 yellow onion, finely chopped
- 25 oz. ground beef or ground lamb/pork
- ½ cup heavy whipping cream
- ½ cup shredded cheese
- 1 egg
- 1 tbsp. dried oregano or dried basil
- 1 tsp salt
- ½ tsp ground black pepper
- 7 oz. sliced bacon
- 1¼ cups heavy whipping cream, for the gravy

Directions:

1. Preheat the oven to 400°F.

2. Fry the onion until it is soft but not overly browned.

3. Mix the ground meat in a bowl with all the other ingredients, minus the bacon. Mix it well, but avoid overworking it as you do not want the mixture to become dense.

4. Mold the meat into a loaf shape and place it in a baking dish. Wrap the loaf completely in the bacon.

5. Bake the loaf in the middle rack of the oven for about 45 minutes. If you notice that the bacon begins to overcook before the meat is done, cover it with some aluminum foil and lower the heat a bit since you do not want burnt bacon.

6. Save all the juices that have accumulated in the baking dish from the meat and bacon, and use to make the gravy. Mix these juices and the cream in a smaller saucepan for the gravy.

7. Bring it to a boil and lower the heat and let it simmer for 10 to 15 minutes until it has the right consistency and is not lumpy.

8. Serve the meatloaf.

9. Serve with freshly boiled broccoli or some cauliflower with butter, salt, and pepper.

Nutrition:

Calories: 308

Protein: 21 Grams

Fat: 8 Grams

Net Carbs: 19 Gram

104. KETO SALMON WITH BROCCOLI MASH

Preparation Time: 20 minutes

Cooking Time: 15 minutes

Servings: 2

Ingredients:

Salmon burgers:

- 1½ lbs. salmon
- 1 egg
- ½ yellow onion
- 1 tsp salt
- ½ tsp pepper
- 2 oz. butter, for frying
- Green mash
- 1 lb. broccoli
- 5 oz. butter
- 2 oz. grated parmesan
- Salt and pepper

Lemon butter:

- 4 oz. butter at room temperature
- 2 tbsp. lemon juice
- Salt and pepper to taste

Directions:

1. Preheat the oven to 220° F. Cut the fish into smaller pieces and place them along with the rest of the ingredients for the burger, into a food processor.

2. Blend it for 30 to 45 seconds until you have a rough mixture. Don't mix it too thoroughly as you do not want tough burgers.

3. Shape 6 to 8 burgers and fry them for 4 to 5 minutes on each side on a medium heat in a generous

amount of butter. Or even oil if you prefer. Keep them warm in the oven.

4. Trim the broccoli and cut it into smaller florets. You can use the stems as well just peel them and chop it into small pieces.

5. Bring a pot of salted water to a boil and add the broccoli to this. Cook it for a few minutes until it is soft, but not until all the texture is gone. Drain and discard the water used for boiling.

6. Use an immersion blender or even a food processor to mix the broccoli with the butter and the parmesan cheese. Season the broccoli mash to taste with salt and pepper.

7. Make the lemon butter by mixing room temperature butter with lemon juice, salt and pepper into a small bowl using electric beaters.

8. Serve the warm burgers with the side of green broccoli mash and a melting dollop of fresh lemon butter on top of the burger.

Nutrition:
Calories: 156
Protein: 15 Grams
Fat: 11 Grams
Net Carbs: 5 Gram

105. OVEN BAKED SAUSAGE AND VEGETABLES

Preparation Time: 10 minutes
Cooking Time: 25 minutes
Servings: 2
Ingredients:

- 1 oz. butter, for greasing the baking dish
- 1 small zucchini
- 2 yellow onions
- 3 garlic cloves
- 51/3 oz. tomatoes
- 7 oz. fresh mozzarella
- Sea salt
- Black pepper
- 1 tbsp. dried basil
- Olive oil
- 1 lb. sausages in links, in links

For Servings:

- 1/2 cup mayonnaise

Directions:

1. Preheat the oven to 400°F. Grease the baking dish with butter.

2. Divide the zucchini into bite-sized pieces. Peel and cut the onion into wedges. Slice or chop the garlic.

3. Place zucchini, onions, garlic, and tomatoes in the baking dish. Dice the cheese and place among the vegetables. Season with salt, pepper and basil.

4. Sprinkle olive oil over the vegetables, and top with sausage.

5. Bake until the sausages are thoroughly cooked and the vegetables are browned.

6. Serve with a dollop of mayonnaise.

Nutrition:
Calories: 176
Protein: 31 Grams
Fat: 12 Grams
Net Carbs: 10 Gram

106. KETO AVOCADO QUICHE

Preparation Time: 15 minutes
Cooking Time: 10 minutes
Servings: 2
Ingredients:

- Pie crust
- ¾ cup almond flour
- 4 tbsp. sesame seeds
- 4 tbsp. coconut flour
- 1 tbsp. ground psyllium husk powder
- 1 tsp baking powder
- 1 pinch salt
- 3 tbsp. olive oil or coconut oil
- 1 egg
- 4 tbsp. water

Filling:

- 2 avocados, ripe
- Mayonnaise
- 3 eggs
- 2tbspfinely chopped fresh cilantro
- 1 finely chopped red chili
- Onion powder
- Salt
- ½ cup cream cheese
- 1¼ cups shredded cheese

Directions:

1. Preheat the oven to 350° F. Mix all the ingredients together for the pie dough in a food processor until the dough forms into a ball, this takes

a few minutes usually. Use your hands or a fork in the absence of a food processor to knead the dough together.

2.　　Place a piece of parchment paper to a spring form pan, no larger than 12 inches around. The spring form pan makes it easier to take the pie out when it is done. Grease the pan and the parchment paper.

3.　　Using an oiled spatula or oil coated fingers, spread the dough into the pan. Bake the crust for 10 minutes.

4.　　Split the avocado in half. Remove the peel and pit it, and dice the avocado.

5.　　Take the seeds out from the chili and chop the chili very finely. Combine the avocado and the chili in a bowl and mix them together with the other ingredients.

6.　　Pour the mixture into the pie crust and bake it for 35 minutes or until it is a light golden brown. Serve it with a green salad.

Nutrition:

Calories: 323

Protein: 45 Grams

Fat: 18 Grams

Net Carbs: 10 Gram

107.　GARLIC CHEDDAR CHICKEN THIGHS

Preparation Time: **5 minutes**

Cooking Time:　**25 minutes**

Servings: **2**

Ingredients:

- 2 chicken thighs
- 1/3 tsp garlic powder
- 1/3 tbsp. dried basil
- 1/3 tbsp. grated cheddar cheese
- 1/2 tsp coconut oil

Seasoning:

- 1/8 tsp salt
- 1/3 tsp ground black pepper

Directions:

1.　　Turn on the oven, then set it to 450°F, and let preheat.

2.　　Meanwhile, prepare the herb mix and for this, stir together 1/4 tsp oil, salt, black pepper, cheese, and basil until combined.

3.　　Create a pocket into each chicken thigh and then stuff it w/ half of the prepared herb mix and spread the remaining herb mix evenly on chicken thighs.

4.　　Take a skillet pan, place it over medium-high heat, add remaining oil and when hot, place stuffed chicken thighs in it and cook for 4 minutes.

5.　　Then flip the chicken thighs, cook for 5 to 7 minutes until the chicken is no longer pink and then roast the chicken thighs for 10 to 12 minutes until a meat thermometer inserted into the thickest part of thighs read 160 degrees F.

6.　　Let chicken thighs rest for 5 minutes and then serve.

Nutrition:

Calories 128.5

Fats 9.5 g

Protein 9 g

Net Carb 0.2 g

Fiber 0.05 g

108.　KETO BUFFALO DRUMSTICKS W/ CHILI AIOLI AND GARLIC

Preparation Time: **10 minutes**

Cooking Time: **40 minutes**

Servings: 2

Ingredients:

- 2 pounds (907g) chicken drumsticks or chicken wings
- 1/3 Cup mayonnaise, keto-friendly
- tbsp. smoked paprika powder or smoked chili powder
- 1 garlic clove, minced
- tbsps. olive oil, and more for greasing the baking dish
- tbsps. white wine vinegar
- 1 tsp. salt
- 1 tsp. paprika powder
- 1 tbsp. tabasco

Directions:

1.　　Now, preheat' the oven to 450°F (235degree C).

2.　　Make the chili aioli: Combine the mayonnaise, smoked paprika powder, garlic clove, olive oil white wine vinegar, salt, paprika powder and tabasco for the marinade in a small bowl,

3.   Put the drumsticks in a plastic bag, and pour the chili aioli into the plastic bag. Shake the bag thoroughly and let marinate for 10 minutes at room temperature.

4.   Coat a baking dish w/ olive oil. Place the drumsticks in the baking dish and let bake in the preheated oven for 30 to 40 minutes or until they are done and have turned a nice color.

5.   Remove the chicken wings from the oven and serve warm.

Nutrition:
Calories: 570
Fat: 43.0g
Total Carbs: 3.0g
Fiber: 1.0g
Protein: 43.0g

109. COLESLAW W/ CRUNCHY KETO CHICKEN THIGHS

Preparation Time: **15 minutes**
Cooking Time: **40 minutes**
Servings: 2
Ingredients:
- tsp. salt
- 1/2 cup sour cream
- tbsps. jerk seasoning (cinnamon, paprika, tumeric, ginger, saffron and cumin)
- lb. (907 g) chicken thighs
- oz. (142 g) pork rinds
- 3 oz. (85 g) unsweetened shredded coconut
- 3 tbsps. olive oil
- 1 lb. (454 g) green cabbage
- 1 cup mayonnaise, keto-friendly
- Salt & freshly ground black pepper, to taste
- 2 big plastic bags

Directions:
1.   Now, preheat' the oven to 350°F (180°C).

2.   Mix together a marinade of jerk seasoning, salt and sour cream. And pour in a big plastic bag w/ the drumsticks, please keep the skin on the drumsticks.

3.   Thoroughly shake and allow to marinate for 15 minutes.

4.   Take the drumsticks out, and into a new, clean bag.

5.   Put the pork rinds into a food processor and blend into fine crumbs, add in coconut flakes and blend a few more seconds.

6.   Pour the pork mixture into the bag w/ the marinated chicken and shake.

7.   Grease a baking dish, and put the chicken into it, drizzle w/ olive oil and bake for 40 to 50 minutes, or until the chicken is cooked through. Turn the drumsticks halfway through, if the breading has already turned a desirable golden brown color, lower the heat.

8.   In the meantime, cut the cabbage finely w/ a sharp knife or w/ a mandolin or even a food processor. Put the coleslaw into a bowl, season w/ salt and pepper, and add mayonnaise, mix well and let sit for 10 minutes.

Nutrition:
Calories: 586
Fat: 51.2g
Total Carbs: 6.4g
Fiber: 2.4g
Protein: 27.2g

110. JERK PORK

Preparation Time: 15 minutes
Cooking Time: 20 minutes
Servings: 2
Ingredients:
- 1/8 tsp. cayenne pepper
- 1/4 tsp. salt
- 1/4 tsp. freshly ground black pepper
- 1/2 tbsp. dried thyme
- 1/2 tbsp. garlic powder
- 1/2 tbsp. ground allspice
- 2tsp. ground cinnamon
- 1 tbsp. granulated erythritol
- 1 (1-pound / 454-g) pork tenderloin, cut into 1-inch rounds
- 1/4 cup extra-virgin olive oil
- 2 tbsps. chopped fresh cilantro, for garnish
- 1/2 cup sour cream

Directions:
1.   Combine the ingredients for the seasoning in a bowl. Stir to mix well.

2.   Put the pork rounds in the bowl of seasoning mixture. Toss to coat well.

3.   Pour the olive oil into a nonstick skillet, and heat over medium-high heat.

4.   Arrange the pork in the singer layer in the skillet and fry for 20 minutes or until an instant-read thermometer inserted in the center of the pork registers at least 145°F (63°C). Flip the pork rounds halfway through the cooking time. You may need to work in batches to avoid overcrowding.

5.   Transfer the pork rounds onto a large platter, and top w/ cilantro and sour cream, then serve warm.

Nutrition:

Calories: 289

Total fat: 23.2g

Total carbs: 2.8g

Fiber: 0.9g

Net carbs: 1.9g

Protein: 17.2g

111.   HOT PORK AND BELL PEPPER IN LETTUCE

Preparation Time: 15 minutes

Cooking Time: 20 minutes

Servings: 2

Ingredients:

SAUCE:

- tbsp. fish sauce
- 1 tbsp. rice vinegar
- 1 tbsp. almond flour
- 1 tsp. coconut aminos
- 1 tbsp. granulated erythritol
- tbsps. coconut oil

PORK FILLING:

- 2 tbsps. sesame oil, divided
- lb. (454 g) ground pork
- 1 tsp. fresh ginger, peeled and grated
- 1 tsp. garlic, minced
- 1 red bell pepper, deseeded and thinly sliced
- 1 scallion, white and green parts, thinly sliced
- 8 large romaine or Boston lettuce leaves

Directions:

1.   Make the sauce: Combine the ingredients for the sauce in a bowl. Set aside until ready to use.

2.   Make the pork filling: In a nonstick skillet, warm a tbsp. sesame oil over medium-high heat.

3.   Add the sauté the ground pork for 8 minutes or until lightly browned, then pour the sauce over

and keep cooking for 4 minutes more or until the sauce has lightly thickened.

4.   Transfer the pork onto a platter and set aside until ready to use.

5.   Clean the skillet w/ paper towels, then warm the remaining sesame oil over medium-high heat.

6.   Add and sauté the ginger and garlic for 3 minutes or until fragrant.

7.   Add and sauté the sliced bell pepper and scallion for an additional 5 minutes or until fork-tender.

8.   Lower the heat, and move the pork back to the skillet. Stir to combine well.

9.   Divide and arrange the pork filling over four lettuce leaves and serve hot.

Nutrition:

Calories: 385

Total fat: 31.1g

Total carbs: 5.8g

Fiber: 1.9g

Net carbs: 3.9g

Protein: 20.1g

112.   LEMONY ANCHOVY BUTTER W/ STEAKS

Preparation Time: 15 minutes

Cooking Time: 10 minutes

Servings: 2

Ingredients:

ANCHOVY BUTTER:

- 4 anchovies packed in oil, drained and minced
- 1/2 tsp. freshly squeezed lemon juice
- 1/4 cup unsalted butter, at room temperature
- tsp. minced garlic
- 4 (4 oz. / 113-g) rib eye steaks
- Salt & freshly ground black pepper, to taste

Directions:

1.   Make the anchovy butter: Combine the anchovies, lemon juice, butter, and garlic in a bowl. Stir to mix well, then arrange the bowl into the refrigerator to chill until ready to use.

2.   Preheat the grill to medium-high heat.

3.   Rub the steaks w/ salt and black pepper on a clean work surface.

4.   Arrange the seasoned steaks on the grill grates and grill for 10 minutes or until medium-rare. Flip steaks halfway through cooking time.

5.   Allow the steaks to cool for 10 minutes. Transfer the steaks onto four plates, and spread the anchovy butter on top, then serve warm.

TIP: To make this a complete meal, you can serve it w/ spicy asparagus. They also taste great paired w/ fresh cucumber salad.

Nutrition:
Calories: 447
Total fat: 38.1g
Total carbs: 0g
Fiber: 0g
Net carbs: 0g
Protein: 26.1g

113.   ZINGY LEMON FISH

Preparation Time: 50 minutes
Cooking Time: 40 minutes
Servings: 2
Ingredients:

- 14 oz. fresh Gurnard fish fillets
- Two tbsps. lemon juice
- Six tbsps. butter
- 1/2 cup fine almond flour
- Two teaspoons dried chives
- One tsp. garlic powder
- Two tsp. dried dill
- Two tsp. onion powder
- Salt and pepper to taste

Directions:
1.   Add almond flour, dried herbs, salt, and spices on a large plate and stir until well combined. Spread it all over the plate evenly.
2.   Place a large pan over medium-high heat. Add half the butter and half the lemon juice. When butter just melts, place fillets on the pan and cook for 3 minutes. Move the fillets around the pan so that it absorbs the butter and lemon juice.
3.   Add remaining half butter and lemon juice. When butter melts, flip sides and cook the other side for 3 minutes.
4.   Serve fillets w/ any butter remaining in the pan.

Nutrition:
Calories 406 Kcal
Fat: 30.33 g
Protein: 29 g
Net carb: 3.55 g

114.   CREAMY   KETO   FISH CASSEROLE

Preparation Time: 1 hour
Cooking Time: 50 minutes
Servings: 2
Ingredients:

- 25 oz. of white fish (slice into bite-sized pieces)
- 15 oz. broccoli (small florets, include the step too)
- 3 oz. butter + extra
- Six scallions (finely chopped)
- 1/4 cups heavy whipping cream
- Two tbsps. small capers
- One tbsp. dried parsley
- One tbsp. Dijon mustard
- 1/4 tsp. black pepper (ground)
- One tsp. salt
- Two tbsps. olive oil
- 5 oz. leafy greens (finely chopped), for garnishing

Directions:
1.   Now, preheat' the oven to 400°F
2.   Now, preheat' the oven oil in a saucepan over medium-high heat.
3.   Fry the broccoli florets in the hot oil for 5 minutes until tender and golden.
4.   Transfer the fried florets to a small bowl and season it w/ salt and pepper. Toss the contents to ensure all the florets get an equal amount of seasoning.
5.   Add the chopped scallions and capers to the same saucepan and fry for 2 minutes. Return the florets to the pan and mix well.
6.   Grease a baking tray w/ a little amount of butter and spread the fried veggies (broccoli, scallions, and capers) in the baking tray.
7.   Add the sliced fish to the tray and nestle it among the veggies.
8.   Mix the heavy cream, mustard, and parsley in a small bowl and pour this mixture over the fish-veggie mixture
9.   Top this w/ the remaining butter and spread gently over the contents using a spatula
10.   Transfer to a plate and garnish w/ chopped greens. Serve warm and enjoy!

Nutrition:
Calories 822
Kcal Fat: 69 g
Protein: 41 g
Net carb: 8 g

115. KETO FISH CASSEROLE W/ MUSHROOMS AND FRENCH MUSTARD

Preparation Time: 1 hour
Cooking Time: 50 minutes
Servings: 2
Ingredients:

- 25 oz. of white fish
- 15 oz. mushrooms (cut into wedges)
- 20 oz. cauliflower (cut into florets)
- 2 cups heavy whipping cream
- 3 oz. butter
- Two tbsps. Dijon mustard
- 3 oz. olive oil
- 8 oz. cheese (shredded)
- Two tbsps. fresh parsley
- Salt & pepper, to taste

Directions:
1. Now, preheat' the oven to 350°F
2. Fry the mushroom for 5 minutes until tender and soft.
3. Add the parsley, salt, and pepper to the mushrooms as you continue to mix well.
4. Reduce the heat and add the mustard and heavy whipping cream to the mushroom.
5. Allow it simmer for 10 minutes until the sauce thickens and reduces a bit.
6. Season the fish slices w/ pepper and salt. Set aside.
7. Sprinkle 3/4th of the cheese over the fish slices and spread the creamy mushroom over the top. Now again, top it w/ the remaining cheese.
8. Boil cauliflower florets in lightly salted water for 5 minutes and strain the water.
9. Place the strained florets in a bowl and add the olive oil. Mash thoroughly w/ a fork until you get a coarse texture—season w/ salt and pepper. Mix well.

Nutrition:
Calories 828
Fat: 71 g

Protein: 39 g
Net carb: 8 g

116. KETO SALMON TANDOORI W/ CUCUMBER SAUCE

Preparation Time: 15 minutes
Cooking Time: 20 minutes
Servings: 2
Ingredients:

- 25 oz. salmon (bite-sized pieces)
- Two tbsps. coconut oil
- One tbsp. tandoori seasoning

For the cucumber sauce

- 1/2 shredded cucumber (squeeze out the water completely)
- Juice of 1/2 lime
- Two minced garlic cloves
- 1/4 cups sour cream or mayonnaise
- 1/2 tsp. salt (optional)

For the crispy salad

- 3 1/2 ounces lettuce (torn)
- Three scallions (finely chopped)
- Two avocados (cubed)
- One yellow bell pepper (diced)
- Juice of 1 lime

Directions:
1. Now, preheat' the oven to 350°F
2. Mix the tandoori seasoning w/ oil in a small bowl and coat the salmon pieces w/ this mixture.
3. Bake for 20 minutes until soft and the salmon flakes w/ a fork
4. Take another bowl and place the shredded cucumber in it. Add the mayonnaise, minced garlic, and salt (if the mayonnaise doesn't have salt) to the shredded cucumber.
5. Mix the lettuce, scallions, avocados, and bell pepper in another bowl. Drizzle the contents w/ the lime juice.
6. Transfer the veggie salad to a plate and place the baked salmon over it. Top the veggies and salmon w/ cucumber sauce.
7. Serve immediately and enjoy!

Nutrition:
Calories 847 Kcal
Fat: 73 g
Protein: 35 g
Net carb: 6 g

117. HERBED SALMON

Preparation Time: 10 minutes
Cooking Time: 8 minutes
Servings: 2
Ingredients:

- 2 garlic cloves, minced
- 1 sp. dried oregano, crushed
- 1 tsp. dried basil, crushed
- Salt and ground black pepper, to taste
- 1/4 cup olive oil
- 2 tbsps. fresh lemon juice
- (4-ounce) salmon fillets

Directions:

1. For salmon: In large bowl, add all ingredients (except salmon) and mix well.
2. Add salmon and coat w/ marinade generously.
3. Cover & refrigerate to marinate for at least 1 hour.
4. Preheat the grill to medium-high heat. Grease the grill grate.
5. Place the salmon in the grill and cook for about 4 minutes per side.
6. Serve hot.

Nutrition:
Calories 263
Net Carbs 0.7 g
Total Fat 19.7 g
Saturated Fat 2.9 g
Cholesterol 50 mg
Sodium 91 mg
Total Carbs 0.9 g
Fiber 0.2 g
Sugar 0.2 g
Protein 22.2 g

118. BUTTERED SALMON

Preparation Time: 10 minutes
Cooking Time: 10 minutes
Servings: 2
Ingredients:

- 4 (5 oz.) skin-on, boneless salmon fillets
- Salt and ground black pepper, to taste
- 1 tbsp. olive oil
- 2 tbsps. butter
- 2 tbsps. lemon juice
- 2 tbsps. fresh rosemary, minced

- 1 tsp. lemon zest, grated

Directions:

1. Season the salmon fillets w/ salt & black pepper evenly.
2. In non-stick wok, heat oil over medium heat.
3. Place salmon fillets, skin side down and cook for about 3–5 minutes, without stirring.
4. Flip the salmon fillets and cook for about 2 minutes.
5. Add the butter, lemon juice, rosemary, and lemon zest, and cook for about 2 minutes, spooning the butter sauce over the salmon fillets occasionally.
6. Serve hot.

Nutrition:
Calories 301
Net Carbs 0.5 g
Total Fat 21.2 g
Saturated Fat 7.4 g
Cholesterol 85 mg
Sodium 165 mg
Total Carbs 1.3 g
Fiber 0.8 g
Sugar 0.2 g
Protein 27.7 g

119. LEMONY SALMON

Preparation Time: 10 minutes
Cooking Time: 10 minutes
Servings: 2
Ingredients:

- 1 tbsp. butter, melted
- 1 tbsp. fresh lemon juice
- 1 tsp. Worcestershire sauce
- 1 tsp. lemon zest, grated finely.
- 4 (6 oz.) salmon fillets
- Salt and ground black pepper, to taste

Directions:

1. In a baking dish, place butter, lemon juice, Worcestershire sauce, and lemon zest, and mix well.
2. Coat the fillets w/ mixture and then arrange skin side-up in the baking dish.
3. Set aside for about 15 minutes.
4. Preheat the broiler of oven.
5. Arrange the oven rack about 6-inch from heating element.
6. Line a broiler pan w/ a piece of foil.
7. Remove the salmon fillets from baking dish and season w/ salt and black pepper.

8.   Arrange the salmon fillets onto the prepared broiler pan, skin side down.
9.   Broil for about 8–10 minutes.
10.   Serve hot.
Nutrition:
Calories 253
Net Carbs 0.3 g
Total Fat 13.4 g
Saturated Fat 34 g
Cholesterol 83 mg
Sodium 149 mg
Total Carbs 0.4 g
Fiber 0.1 g
Sugar 0.4 g
Protein 33.1 g

120.   CHEESY TILAPIA
Preparation Time: 10 minutes
Cooking Time: 15 minutes
Servings: 2
Ingredients:
- 2 pounds tilapia fillets
- 1/2 cup Parmesan cheese, grated
- 3 tbsps. mayonnaise
- 1/4 cup unsalted butter, softened
- 2 tbsps. fresh lemon juice
- 1/4 tsp. dried thyme, crushed
- Salt and ground black pepper, to taste

Directions:
1.   Preheat the broiler of oven.
2.   Grease a broiler pan.
3.   In a large bowl, mix the ingredients except tilapia fillets. Set aside.
4.   Place the fillets onto prepared broiler pan in a single layer.
5.   Broil the fillets for about 2–3 minutes.
6.   Remove the broiler pan from oven and top the fillets w/ cheese mixture evenly.
7.   Broil for about 2 minutes further.
8.   Serve hot.
Nutrition:
Calories 185
Net Carb 1.4 g
Total Fat 9.8 g
Saturated Fat 5 g
Cholesterol 76 mg
Sodium 183 mg
Total Carbs 1.4 g

Fiber 0 g
Sugar 0.4 g
Protein 23.2 g

121.   ROASTED MACKEREL
Preparation Time: 10 minutes
Cooking Time: 20 minutes
Servings: 2
Ingredients:
- 2 (7 oz.) mackerel fillets
- 1 tbsp. butter, melted
- Salt and ground black pepper, to taste

Directions:
1.   Now, preheat' the oven to 350°F.
2.   Arrange a rack, in the middle of oven.
3.   Lightly, grease a baking dish.
4.   Brush the fish fillets w/ melted butter and then season w/ salt and black pepper.
5.   Arrange the fish fillets into the prepared baking dish in a single layer.
6.   Bake for about 20 minutes.
7.   Serve hot.
Nutrition:
Calories 571
Net Carbs 0 g
Total Fat 41.1 g
Saturated Fat 11.9 g
Cholesterol 164 mg
Sodium 283 mg
Total Carbs 0 g
Fiber 0 g
Sugar 0 g
Protein 47.4 g

122.   PORK CUTLETS W/ SPANISH ONION
Preparation Time: 15 minutes
Cooking Time: 15 minutes
Servings: 2
Ingredients:
- 1 tbsp. olive oil
- pork cutlets
- 1 bell pepper, deveined and sliced
- 1 Spanish onion, chopped
- garlic cloves, minced
- 1/2 tsp. hot sauce
- 1/2 tsp. mustard
- 1/2 tsp. paprika

- Kitchen Equipment:
- saucepan

Directions:

1. Fry the pork cutlets for 3 to 4 minutes until evenly golden and crispy on both sides.
2. Set the temperature to medium and add the bell pepper, Spanish onion, garlic, hot sauce, and mustard; continue cooking until the vegetables have softened, for a further 3 minutes.
3. Sprinkle w/ paprika, salt, and black pepper. Serve immediately and enjoy!

Nutrition:

403 Calories

24.1g Fat

3.4g Total Carbs

123. RICH AND EASY PORK RAGOUT

Preparation Time: 15 minutes

Cooking Time: 15 minutes

Servings: 2

Ingredients:

- 1 tsp. lard, melted at room temperature
- 3/4-lb. pork butt, cut into bite-sized cubes
- 1 red bell pepper, deveined and chopped
- 1 poblano pepper, deveined and chopped
- cloves garlic, pressed
- 1/2 cup leeks, chopped
- 1/2 tsp. mustard seeds
- 1/4 tsp. ground allspice
- 1/4 tsp. celery seeds
- 1 cup roasted vegetable broth
- vine-ripe tomatoes, pureed
- Kitchen Equipment:
- Stockpot

Directions:

1. Melt the lard in a stockpot over moderate heat. Once hot, cook the pork cubes for 4 to 6 minutes, occasionally stirring to ensure even cooking.
2. Then, stir in the vegetables and continue cooking until they are tender and fragrant. Add in the salt, black pepper, mustard seeds, allspice, celery seeds, roasted vegetable broth, and tomatoes.
3. Reduce the heat to simmer. Let it simmer for 30 minutes longer or until everything is heated through. Ladle into individual bowls and serve hot. Bon appétit!

Nutrition:

389 Calories

24.3g Fat

5.4g Total Carbs

124. PULLED PORK W/ MINT AND CHEESE

Preparation Time: 20 minutes

Cooking Time: 15 minutes

Servings: 2

Ingredients:

- 1 tsp. lard, melted at room temperature
- 3/4 pork Boston butt, sliced
- garlic cloves, pressed
- 1/2 tsp. red pepper flakes, crushed
- 1/2 tsp. black peppercorns, freshly cracked
- Sea salt, to taste
- bell peppers, deveined and sliced
- 1 tbsp. fresh mint leave snipped
- 2 tbsps. cream cheese
- Kitchen Equipment:
- cast-iron skillet

Directions:

1. Melt the lard in a cast-iron skillet over a moderate flame. Once hot, brown the pork for 2 minutes per side until caramelized and crispy on the edges.
2. Set the temperature to medium-low and continue cooking for another 4 minutes, turning over periodically. Shred the pork w/ two forks and return to the skillet.
3. Add the garlic, red pepper, black peppercorns, salt, and bell pepper and continue cooking for a further 2 minutes or until the peppers are just tender and fragrant.
4. Serve w/ fresh mint and a dollop of cream cheese. Enjoy!

Nutrition:

370 Calories

21.9g Fat

34.9g Protein

125. FESTIVE MEATLOAF

Preparation Time: 1 hour

Cooking Time: 50 minutes

Servings: 2

Ingredients:

- ¼lb. ground pork
- ½ lb. ground chuck
- 2 eggs, beaten
- 1/4 cup flaxseed meal
- shallot, chopped
- garlic cloves, minced
- 1/2 tsp. smoked paprika
- 1/4 tsp. dried basil
- 1/4 tsp. ground cumin
- Kosher salt, to taste
- 1/2 cup tomato puree
- tsp. mustard
- 1 tsp. liquid monk fruit
- Kitchen Equipment:
- mixing bowl
- loaf pan
- oven

Directions:

1. In a bowl, mix the ground meat, eggs, flaxseed meal, shallot, garlic, and spices thoroughly.
2. In another bowl, mix the tomato puree w/ the mustard and liquid monk fruit, whisk to combine well.
3. Press the mixture into the loaf pan—Bake in the preheated oven at 360°F for 30 minutes.

Nutrition:
517 Calories
32.3g Fat
48.5g Protein

126. RICH WINTER BEEF STEW

Preparation Time: 45 minutes
Cooking Time: 50 minutes
Servings: 2
Ingredients:

- 1-oz. bacon, diced
- ¾ lb. well-marbled beef chuck, boneless and cut into 1- 1/2-inch pieces
- red bell pepper, chopped
- green bell pepper, chopped
- garlic cloves, minced
- 1/2 cup leeks, chopped
- parsnip, chopped
- Sea salt, to taste

- 1/4 tsp. mixed peppercorns, freshly cracked
- cups of chicken bone broth
- 1 tomato, pureed
- cups kale, torn into pieces
- 1 tbsp. fresh cilantro, roughly chopped
- Kitchen Equipment:
- Dutch pot

Directions:

1. Heat a Dutch pot over medium-high flame. Now, cook the bacon until it is well browned and crisp; reserve. Then, cook the beef pieces for 3 to 5 minutes or until just browned on all sides; reserve. After that, sauté the peppers, garlic, leeks, and parsnip in the pan drippings until they are just tender and aromatic. Add the salt, peppercorns, chicken bone broth, tomato, and reserved beef to the pot. Bring to a boil. Stir in the kale leaves and continue simmering until the leaves have wilted or 3 to 4 minutes more.
2. Ladle into individual bowls & serve garnished w/ fresh cilantro and the reserved bacon.

Nutrition:
359 Calories
17.8g Fat
1g Fiber

127. CRISPY TILAPIA

Preparation Time: 15 minutes
Cooking Time: 14 minutes
Servings: 2
Ingredients:

- ¾ cup pork rinds, crushed
- 1 packet dry ranch-style dressing mix
- 2½ tbsp. olive oil
- 2 organic eggs
- 4 tilapia fillets

Directions:

1. Arrange the greased Cook & Crisp Basket in the pot of Ninja Foodi.
2. Close the Ninja Foodi with crisping lid and select Air Crisp.
3. Set the temperature to 355 degrees F for 5 minutes.
4. Press "Start/Stop" to begin preheating.
5. In a shallow bowl, beat the eggs.

6.	In another bowl, add the pork rinds, ranch dressing, and oil and mix until a crumbly mixture form.
7.	Put the fish fillets into the egg then coat with the pork rind mixture.
8.	After preheating, open the lid.
9.	Arrange the tilapia fillets in the prepared Cook & Crisp Basket in a single layer.
10.	Close the Ninja Foodi with crisping lid and select Air Crisp.
11.	Set the temperature to 350°F for 14 minutes.
12.	Press Start/Stop to begin cooking.
13.	Serve hot.
Nutrition:
Calories: 304
Fats: 16.8g
Carbohydrates 0.4 g
Proteins: 38g

## 128.	COD WITH TOMATOES

Preparation Time: 15 minutes
Cooking Time: 16 minutes
Servings: 2
Ingredients:
•	1-pound cherry tomatoes halved
•	2 tablespoons fresh rosemary, chopped
•	4 cod fillets
•	2 garlic cloves, minced
•	1 tbsp. olive oil
•	Salt and ground black pepper
Directions:
1.	At the bottom of a greased a large heatproof bowl, place half of the cherry tomatoes followed by the rosemary.
2.	Arrange cod fillets on top in a single layer, followed by the remaining tomatoes.
3.	Sprinkle with garlic and drizzle with oil.
4.	At the bottom of Ninja Foodie, arrange the bowl.
5.	Close the Ninja Foodi with the pressure lid and place the pressure valve to Seal position.
6.	Select Pressure and set to High for 6 minutes.
7.	Press Start/Stop to begin cooking.
8.	Switch the valve to Vent and do a quick release.
9.	Transfer the fish fillets and tomatoes onto serving plates.
10.	Sprinkle with salt and black pepper and serve.

Nutrition:
Calories: 149
Fats: 5g
Carbohydrates 6 g
Proteins: 21.4g

## 129.	CRAB CASSEROLE

Preparation Time: 10 minutes
Cooking Time: 30 minutes
Servings: 2
Ingredients:
•	2 tbsp. of oil, for frying
•	1 onion, finely chopped
•	150 g finely chopped celery stalks
•	salt and pepper
•	300 ml homemade mayonnaise
•	4 eggs
•	450 g canned crab meat
•	325 g grated white cheddar cheese
•	2 tsp. paprika
•	¼ tsp. cayenne pepper
For filing
•	75 g leafy greens
•	2 tbsp. of olive oil
Directions:
1.	Set the oven to 350°F. Grease a 9x12 baking dish.
2.	Fry onion and celery in oil until translucent.
3.	In another bowl, add mayonnaise, eggs, crab meat, seasonings, and 2/3 chopped cheese. Add the fried onions and celery and stir.
4.	Add the mass to the baking dish. Sprinkle the remaining cheese on top and bake for about 30 minutes or until golden brown.
5.	Serve with salad and olive oil.
Nutrition:
Carbohydrates: 6 g
Fats: 95 g
Proteins: 47 g
Calories: 400

## 130.	SALMON SKEWERS IN CURED HAM

Preparation Time: 10 minutes
Cooking Time: 15 minutes
Servings: 2
Ingredients:

- Salmon Skewers
- 60 ml finely chopped fresh basil
- 450 g salmon
- salt black pepper
- 100 g dried ham sliced
- 1 tbsp. l Olive oil
- 8 pcs wooden skewers
- Innings
- 225 ml mayonnaise

Directions:
1. Soak the skewers in water.
2. Finely chop fresh basil.
3. Cut salmon fillet into rectangular pieces and fasten on skewers.
4. Roll each kebab in the basil and pepper.
5. Cut the cured ham into thin slices and wrap her every kebab.
6. Lubricate with olive oil and fry on in a pan, grill, or in the oven.
7. Serve with mayonnaise or salad

Nutrition:
Carbohydrates: 1 g
Fats: 62 g
Proteins: 28 g
Calories: 680

131. CHEESY CHICKEN SUN-DRIED TOMATO PACKETS

Preparation Time: 15 minutes
Cooking Time: 40 minutes
Servings: 2
Ingredients:
- 1 cup goat cheese
- ½ cup chopped oil-packed sun-dried tomatoes
- 1 tsp. minced garlic
- ½ tsp. dried basil
- ½ tsp. dried oregano
- 4 (4 oz.) boneless chicken breasts
- Sea salt, for seasoning
- Freshly ground black pepper, for seasoning
- 3 tbsp. olive oil

Directions:
1. Preheat the oven. Set the oven temperature to 375°F.

2. Prepare the filling. In a medium bowl, put the goat cheese, sun-dried tomatoes, garlic, basil, and oregano then mix until everything is well blended.
3. Stuff the chicken. Make a horizontal slice in the middle of each chicken breast to make a pocket, making sure not to cut through the sides or ends. Spoon one-quarter of the filling into each breast, folding the skin and chicken meat over the slit to form packets. Secure the packets with a toothpick. Lightly season the breasts with salt and pepper.
4. Brown the chicken. In a large oven-safe skillet over medium heat, warm the olive oil. Add the breasts and sear them, turning them once, until they are golden, about 8 minutes in total.
5. Bake the chicken. Bring the skillet into the oven and bake the chicken for 30 minutes or until it's cooked through.
6. Serve. Remove the toothpicks. Divide the chicken into 4 plates and serve them immediately.

Nutrition:
Calories: 388
Total fat: 29g
Total carbs: 4g
Fiber: 1g;
Net carbs: 3g
Protein: 28g

132. TUSCAN CHICKEN SAUTÉ

Preparation Time: 10 minutes
Cooking Time: 35 minutes
Servings: 2
Ingredients:
- 1 lb. boneless chicken breasts, each cut into three pieces
- Sea salt, for seasoning
- Freshly ground black pepper, for seasoning
- 3 tbsp. olive oil
- 1 tbsp. minced garlic
- ¾ cup chicken stock
- 1 tsp. dried oregano
- ½ tsp. dried basil
- ½ cup heavy (whipping) cream
- ½ cup shredded Asiago cheese
- 1 cup fresh spinach
- ¼ cup sliced Kalamata olives

Directions:

1.	Prepare the chicken. Pat, the chicken, breasts dry and lightly season them with salt and pepper.
2.	Sauté the chicken. In a large skillet over medium-high heat, warm the olive oil. Add the chicken and sauté until it is golden brown and just cooked through, about 15 minutes in total. Transfer the chicken to a plate and set it aside.
3.	Make the sauce. Put the garlic to the skillet, then sauté until it's softened about 2 minutes. Stir in the chicken stock, oregano, and basil, scraping up any browned bits in the skillet. Bring to a boil, then reduce the heat to low and simmer until the sauce is reduced by about one-quarter, about 10 minutes.
4.	Finish the dish. Stir in the cream, Asiago, and simmer, stirring the sauce frequently, until it has thickened about 5 minutes. Put back the chicken to the skillet along with any accumulated juices. Stir in the spinach and olives and simmer until the spinach is wilted about 2 minutes.
5.	Serve. Divide the chicken and sauce between four plates and serve it immediately.
Nutrition:
Calories: 483
Total fat: 38g
Total carbs: 5g
Fiber: 1g;
Net carbs: 3g
Protein: 31g

## 133.	LAMB LEG WITH SUN-DRIED TOMATO PESTO

Preparation Time: 15 minutes
Cooking Time: 70 minutes
Servings: 2
Ingredients:
For the Pesto:
•	1 cup sun-dried tomatoes packed in oil
•	¼ cup pine nuts
•	2 tbsp. extra-virgin olive oil
•	2 tbsp. chopped fresh basil
•	2 tsp. minced garlic
For the Lamb Leg:
•	1 (2-lb.) lamb leg
•	Sea salt
•	Freshly ground black pepper
•	2 tbsp. olive oil
Directions:

To make the Pesto:
1.	Place the sun-dried tomatoes, pine nuts, olive oil, basil, and garlic in a blender or food processor; process until smooth.
2.	Set aside until needed.
To make the Lamb Leg
3.	Preheat the oven to 400°F.
4.	Season the lamb leg all over with salt and pepper.
5.	Bring a large ovenproof skillet over medium-high heat and add the olive oil.
6.	Sear the lamb on all sides until nicely browned, about 6 minutes in total.
7.	Spread the sun-dried tomato pesto all over the lamb and place the lamb on a baking sheet. Roast
8.	Let the lamb rest for 10 minutes before slicing and serving.
Nutrition:
Calories: 352
Fat: 29g
Protein: 17g
Carbs: 5g
Fiber: 2g
Net Carbs: 3g

## 134.	ONE-SKILLET GREEN PASTA

Preparation Time: 10 minutes
Cooking Time: 5 minutes
Servings: 2
Ingredients:
•	1 cup shredded mozzarella cheese
•	1 cup grated Pecorino Romano cheese for topping
•	1 egg yolk
•	2 garlic cloves, minced
•	1 lemon, juiced
•	1 cup baby spinach
•	½ cup almond milk
•	1 avocado, pitted and peeled
•	1 tbsp. olive oil
•	Salt to taste
Directions:
1.	Microwave mozzarella cheese for 2 minutes.
2.	Take out the bowl and allow cooling for 1 minute. Mix in egg yolk until well-combined.

3. Lay a parchment paper on a flat surface, pour the cheese mixture on top, and cover it with another parchment paper.
4. Flatten the dough into 1/8-inch thickness.
5. Take off the parchment paper and cut the dough into thick fettuccine strands. Place in a bowl and refrigerate overnight.
6. Place 2 cups water to a boil in a saucepan and add the fettuccine.
7. Cook for 1 minute and drain; set aside. In a blender, combine garlic, lemon juice, spinach, almond milk, avocado, olive oil, and salt. Process until smooth. Pour fettuccine into a bowl, top with sauce, and mix.
8. Top with Pecorino Romano cheese and serve.
Nutrition:
Calories 290
Net Carbs 5g
Fats 19g
Protein 18g

135. CHARRED ASPARAGUS WITH CREAMY SAUCE

Preparation Time: 5 minutes
Cooking Time: 7 minutes
Servings: 2
Ingredients:
- ½ lb. asparagus, no hard stalks
- Salt and chili pepper to taste
- 4 tbsp. flax seed powder
- ½ cup coconut cream
- 1 cup butter, melted
- 1/3 cup mozzarella, grated
- 2 tbsp. olive oil
- Juice of half lemon

Directions:
1. Warm olive oil in a saucepan then roast the asparagus until lightly charred.
2. Season with salt and set aside.
3. Melt half of butter in a pan and stir until nutty and golden brown.
4. Add in lemon juice and pour the mixture over the asparagus. In a safe microwave bowl, mix flax seed powder with ½ cup water and let sit for 5 minutes.
5. Microwave flax egg 1-2 minutes, then pour into a blender.

6. Add the remaining butter, mozzarella cheese, coconut cream, salt, and chili pepper.
7. Puree until well combined and smooth. Serve.
Nutrition:
Calories 442
Net Carbs 5.4g
Fat 45g
Protein 5.9g

136. SWEET ONION & GOAT CHEESE PIZZA

Preparation Time: 10 minutes
Cooking Time: 40 minutes
Servings: 2
Ingredients:
- 2 cups grated mozzarella
- 2 tbsp. cream cheese, softened
- 2 large eggs, beaten
- 1/3 cup almond flour
- 1 tsp dried Italian seasoning
- 2 tbsps. butter
- 2 red onions, thinly sliced
- 1 cup crumbled goat cheese
- 1 tbsp. almond milk
- 1 cup curly endive, chopped

Directions:
1. Set the oven to 390°F. Line a round pizza pan using parchment paper. Microwave the mozzarella and cream cheeses for 1 minute. Remove and mix in eggs, almond flour, and Italian seasoning.
2. Spread On the pizza pan, spread the dough then bake for 6 minutes. Melt butter in a skillet, then onions, salt, and pepper and cook on low heat with frequent stirring until caramelized, 15-20 minutes. In a bowl, mix goat cheese with almond milk and spread on the crust. Top with the caramelized onions. Bake for 10 minutes. Scatter curly endive on top, slice, and serve.
Nutrition:
Calories 317
Net Carbs 3g
Fats 20g
Protein 28g

137. GRILLED CALAMARI

Preparation Time: 10 minutes
Cooking Time: 5 minutes
Servings: 2
Ingredients:
- 2 pounds calamari tubes and tentacles, cleaned
- ½ cup good-quality olive oil
- Zest and juice of 2 lemons
- 2 tbsp. chopped fresh oregano
- 1 tbsp. minced garlic
- ¼ tsp. sea salt
- 1/8 tsp. freshly ground black pepper

Directions:
1. Prepare the calamari. Score the top layer of the calamari tubes about 2 inches apart.
2. Marinate the calamari.
3. In a large bowl, stir together the olive oil, lemon zest, lemon juice, oregano, garlic, salt, and pepper.
4. Add the calamari and toss to coat it well, then place it in the refrigerator to marinate for at least 30 minutes to 1 hour. Grill the calamari. Preheat a grill to high heat. Grill the calamari, turning once, for about 3 minutes total, until it's tender and lightly charred.
5. Serve. Divide the calamari between four plates and serve it hot.

Nutrition:
Calories: 455
Total fat: 30g
Total carbs: 8g
Fiber: 1g;
Net carbs: 7g
Protein: 35g

138. PROSCUITTO-WRAPPED HADDOCK

Preparation Time: 10 minutes
Cooking Time: 15 minutes
Servings: 2
Ingredients:
- 4 (4-oz.) haddock fillets, about 1 inch thick
- Sea salt, for seasoning
- Freshly ground black pepper, for seasoning
- 4 slices prosciutto (2oz.)
- 3 tbsp. garlic-infused olive oil
- Juice and zest of 1 lemon

Directions:
1. Preheat the oven. Set the oven temperature to 350°F. Line a baking sheet with parchment paper.
2. Prepare the fish. Pat the fish dry using paper towels then spice it lightly on both sides with salt and pepper. Wrap the prosciutto around the fish tightly but carefully so it doesn't rip.
3. Bake the fish. Bring the fish on the baking sheet and drizzle it with the olive oil. Bake for 15 to 17 minutes until the fish flakes easily with a fork.
4. Serve. Divide the fish between four plates and top with the lemon zest and a drizzle of lemon juice.

Nutrition:
Calories: 282
Total fat: 18g
Total carbs: 1g
Fiber: 0g;
Net carbs: 1g
Protein: 29g

139. GRILLED SALMON WITH CAPONATA

Preparation Time: 15 minutes
Cooking Time: 20 minutes
Servings: 2
Ingredients:
- ¼ cup good-quality olive oil, divided
- 1 onion, chopped
- 2 celery stalks, chopped
- 1 tbsp. minced garlic
- 2 tomatoes, chopped
- ½ cup chopped marinated artichoke hearts
- ¼ cup pitted green olives, chopped
- ¼ cup cider vinegar
- 2 tbsp. white wine
- 2 tbsp. chopped pecans
- 4 (4-oz.) salmon fillets
- Freshly ground black pepper, for seasoning
- 2 tsp. chopped fresh basil

Directions:
1. Make the caponata. In a large skillet at medium heat, warm 3 tablespoons of the olive oil.
2. Add the onion, celery, garlic, and sauté until they have softened, about 4 minutes.

3. Stir in the tomatoes, artichoke hearts, olives, vinegar, white wine, and pecans.

4. Place the mixture to a boil, then reduce the heat to low and simmer until the liquid has reduced, 6 to 7 minutes. Take off the skillet from the heat and set it aside.

5. Grill the fish. Preheat a grill to medium-high heat.

6. Pat the fish dry using paper towels then rub it with the remaining 1 tablespoon of olive oil and season lightly with black pepper. Grill the salmon, turning once, until it is just cooked through, about 8 minutes total.

7. Serve. Divide the salmon between four plates, top with a generous scoop of the caponata, and serve immediately with fresh basil.

Nutrition:
Calories: 348
Total fat: 25g
Total carbs: 7g
Fiber: 3g
Net carbs: 4g
Protein: 24g

140. SWEET CRAB CAKES

Preparation Time: 15 minutes
Cooking Time: 10 minutes
Servings: 2
Ingredients:
- 1 lb. cooked lump crabmeat, drained and picked over
- ¼ cup shredded unsweetened coconut
- 1 tablespoon Dijon mustard
- 1 scallion, finely chopped
- ¼ cup minced red bell pepper
- 1 egg, lightly beaten
- 1 teaspoon lemon zest
- Pinch cayenne pepper
- 3 tbsp. coconut flour
- 3 tbsp. coconut oil
- ¼ cup classic aioli

Directions:
1. Make the crab cakes. In a medium bowl, mix the crab, coconut, mustard, scallion, red bell pepper, egg, lemon zest, and cayenne until it holds together. Form the mixture into eight equal patties about ¾ inch thick.

2. Chill. Place the patties on a plate, cover the plate with plastic wrap, and chill them in the refrigerator for around 1 hour to 12 hours.

3. Coat the patties. Spread the coconut flour on a plate. Dip each patty in the flour until it is lightly coated.

4. Cook. In a large skillet at medium heat, warm the coconut oil. Fry the crab-cake patties, turning them once, until they are golden and cooked through, about 5 minutes per side.

5. Serve. Place two crab cakes on each of four plates and serve with the aioli.

Nutrition:
Calories: 370
Total fat: 24g
Total carbs: 12g
Fiber: 6g
Net carbs: 6g
Protein: 26g

141. RED PEPPER AND MOZZARELLA-STUFFED CHICKEN CAPRESE

Preparation Time: 10 minutes
Cooking Time: 40 minutes
Servings: 2
Ingredients:
- 2 tbsp. extra-virgin olive oil
- 2 chicken breasts, butterflied
- 10 fresh basil leaves
- 1 (8-oz.) ball mozzarella cheese, cut into 4 pieces
- 1 cup Roasted Red Peppers
- 2 tbsp. Italian seasoning
- Sea salt
- Freshly ground black pepper

Directions:
1. Preheat the oven to 400°F.

2. Line a rimmed baking sheet using a parchment paper.

3. Place 5 basil leaves inside each chicken breast.

4. Place 2 mozzarella slices inside each breast.

5. Divide the roasted red peppers into 2 breasts. Sprinkle the Italian seasoning generously over each breast and season them with salt and pepper. Close each breast to envelop the filling.

6.	Put the breasts on the baking sheet and bake until cooked through about 40 minutes. Serve hot.

Nutrition:
Calories: 539
Total Fat: 30g
Protein: 63g
Carbohydrates: 4g
Fiber: 1g
Net Carbs: 3g

142. LEMON-GARLIC CHICKEN AND GREEN BEANS WITH CARAMELIZED ONIONS

Preparation Time: 10 minutes
Cooking Time: 65 minutes
Servings: 2
Ingredients:

- 3 tbsp. extra-virgin olive oil
- 3 tbsp. freshly squeezed lemon juice
- 2 tbsp. minced garlic
- 1 tsp. sea salt, plus additional for seasoning
- ¼ tsp. Freshly ground black pepper
- ¼ tsp. paprika
- 1/8 tsp. red pepper flakes
- 2 large boneless, skinless free-range chicken breasts
- 1 yellow onion, quartered
- 2 cups trimmed green beans
- ¼ cup Golden Ghee, melted

Directions:
1.	In .a medium bowl or a zipper-top plastic bag, combine the olive oil, lemon juice, garlic, salt, black pepper, paprika, and red pepper flakes.
2.	Put the chicken then coat it in the marinade.
3.	Cover the bowl or seal the bag then marinate the chicken in the fridge for at least 1 hour, or overnight if possible.
4.	Preheat the oven to 350°F.
5.	Dice 1 of the onion quarters, and cut the remaining 3 quarters into large chunks.
6.	Put the larger chunks of onion across the bottom of a cast iron or ovenproof skillet.
7.	Put the green beans, then scatter the diced onion above. Place on the top the green beans and onion with the ghee. Put the marinated chicken breasts on the green beans then spoon the remaining

marinade at the chicken. Season the dish with a sprinkle of sea salt.
8.	Bake the chicken until its internal temperature reaches at least 165°F, about 65 minutes. Serve hot.

Nutrition:
Calories: 803
Total Fat: 61g
Protein: 53g
Carbohydrates: 14g
Fiber: 5g
Net Carbs: 9g

143. THREE-CHEESE CHICKEN CORDON BLEU

Preparation Time: 10minutes
Cooking Time: 50 minutes
Servings: 2
Ingredients:

- ½ cup shredded organic Gruyère cheese
- ½ cup shredded organic Emmentaler (Swiss) cheese
- ¼ cup shredded organic Appenzeller cheese
- 1/8 tsp. ground nutmeg
- 2 large boneless, skinless, free-range chicken breasts, butterflied and pounded thin
- 4 slices nitrate-free ham
- 2 tsp. Dijon mustard (optional)
- 1 tbsp extra-virgin olive oil
- ½ cup grated organic Parmesan cheese
- ½ teaspoon Seasoned Salt (here)

Directions:
1.	Preheat the oven to 375°F.
2.	Line a rimmed baking sheet using parchment paper.
3.	In a small bowl, combine the Gruyère, Emmentaler, and Appenzeller cheeses with the nutmeg.
4.	Lay the butterflied chicken breasts flat on a work surface and divide the cheese mixture between the two breasts.
5.	Then place 2 slices of ham on top of the cheese on each breast, followed by 1 teaspoon of Dijon mustard in the middle (if using). Fold the chicken breast over to enclose the filling.

6. Brush the olive oil into a chicken, and sprinkle it with the Parmesan cheese and seasoned salt.

7. Place the stuffed chicken breasts on the baking sheet and bake until the internal temperature reaches at least 165°F, about 50 minutes. Serve hot.

Nutrition:

Calories: 848

Total Fat: 52g

Protein: 88g

Carbohydrates: 4g

Fiber: 1g

Net Carbs: 3g

144. BACON WRAPPED-BEEF TENDERLOIN

Preparation Time: 10 minutes

Cooking Time: 15 minutes

Servings: 2

Ingredients:

- 4 (4 oz.) beef tenderloin steaks
- Sea salt
- Freshly ground black pepper
- 8 bacon slices
- 1 tablespoon extra-virgin olive oil

Directions:

1. Preheat the oven to 450°F.

2. Season the steaks with salt and pepper.

3. Wrap each steak snugly around the edges with 2 slices of bacon and secure the bacon with toothpicks.

4. Bring a large skillet at medium-high heat and add the olive oil.

5. Pan sear the steaks for 4 minutes per side and transfer them to a baking sheet.

6. Roast the steaks until they reach your desired doneness, about 6 minutes for medium.

7. Remove the steaks from the oven and let them rest for 10 minutes.

8. Remove the toothpicks and serve.

Nutrition:

Calories: 565

Fat: 49g

Protein: 28g

Carbs: 0g

Fiber: 0g

Net Carbs: 0g

145. CHEESEBURGER CASSEROLE

Preparation Time: 10 minutes

Cooking Time: 40 minutes

Servings: 2

Ingredients:

- 1 lb. 75% lean ground beef
- ½ cup chopped sweet onion
- 2 tsp. minced garlic
- 1½ cups shredded aged Cheddar, divided
- ½ cup heavy (whipping) cream
- 1 large tomato, chopped
- 1 tsp. minced fresh basil
- ¼ tsp. sea salt
- 1/8 tsp. freshly ground black pepper

Directions:

1. Preheat the oven to 350°F.

2. Set a large skillet at medium-high heat and add the ground beef.

3. Brown the beef until cooked through, about 6 minutes, and spoon off any excess fat.

4. Stir in the onion and garlic and cook until the vegetables are tender about 4 minutes.

5. Transfer the beef and vegetables to an 8-by-8-inch casserole dish.

6. In a medium bowl, place 1 cup of shredded cheese and the heavy cream, tomato, basil, salt, and pepper then mix until well combined.

7. Pour the cream mixture over the beef mixture and top the casserole with the remaining ½ cup of shredded cheese.

8. Bake until the casserole is bubbly and the cheese is melted and lightly browned, about 30 minutes.

9. Serve.

Nutrition:

Calories: 410

Fat: 33g

Protein: 20g

Carbs: 3g

Fiber: 0g

Net Carbs: 3g

CHAPTER 8.   DESSERTS

146.   SPICY PECANS

Preparation Time: 10 minutes
Cooking Time: 3 hours
Servings: 2
Ingredients:
- lbs. pecan halves
- tbsp. Cajun seasoning blend
- tbsp. olive oil

Directions:
1. Add all ingredients to the slow cooker and stir well to combine.
2. Cover slow cooker with lid and cook on low for 1 hour.
3. Stir well. Cover again and cook for 2 hours more.
4. Serve and enjoy.

Nutrition:
Calories 607
Fat 62.5 g
Carbohydrates 12.2 g
Sugar 3 g
Protein 9.1 g
Cholesterol 0 mg

147.   TASTY SEASONED MIXED NUTS

Preparation Time: 10 minutes
Cooking Time: 2 hours
Servings: 20
Ingredients:
- cups mixed nuts
- tbsp. curry powder
- tbsp. butter, melted
- Salt

Directions:
1. Add all ingredients into the slow cooker and stir well to combine.
2. Cover slow cooker with lid and cook on high for a ½ hour. Stir again and cook for 30 minutes more.
3. Cover again and cook on low for 1 hour more.
4. Stir well and serve.

Nutrition:
Calories 375
Fat 34.7 g
Carbohydrates 12.8 g
Sugar 2.5 g

Protein 9 g
Cholesterol 6 mg

148.   NACHO CHEESE DIP

Preparation Time: 10 minutes
Cooking Time: 2 hours
Servings: 2
Ingredients:
- oz. cream cheese, cut into chunks
- ¼ cup almond milk
- ½ cup chunky salsa
- 1 cup cheddar cheese, shredded

Directions:
1. Add all ingredients to the slow cooker and stir well.
2. Cover slow cooker with lid and cook on low for 2 hours. Stir to mix.
3. Serve with fresh vegetables.

Nutrition:
Calories 178
Fat 16.4 g
Carbohydrates 2.4 g
Sugar 0.9 g
Protein 6.1 g
Cholesterol 46 mg

149.   EASY TEXAS DIP

Preparation Time: 10 minutes
Cooking Time: 6 hours
Servings: 2
Ingredients:
- 1 ½ cups Velveeta cheese, cubed
- cups fresh tomatoes, diced
- oz. can green chilies, diced
- 1 large onion, chopped

Directions:
1. Add all ingredients into the slow cooker and stir well to combine.
2. Cover slow cooker with lid and cook on low for 6 hours.
3. Stir well and serve.

Nutrition:
Calories 104
Fat 7.2 g
Carbohydrates 4.4 g
Sugar 2.1 g
Protein 6 g
Cholesterol 22 mg

150.   CHEESE CHICKEN DIP

Preparation Time: 10 minutes
Cooking Time: 2 hours
Servings: 2
Ingredients:
* ½ cup bell peppers, chopped
* 1 cup chicken breast, cooked and shredded
* oz. can tomato with green chilies
* ½ lb. cheese, cubed

Directions:
1.   Add all ingredients into the slow cooker and stir well to combine.
2.   Cover slow cooker with lid and cook on low for 2 hours.
3.   Stir well and serve.

Nutrition:
Calories 120
Fat 8 g
Carbohydrates 2 g
Sugar 0.4 g
Protein 10 g

151.   FLAVORFUL   MEXICAN CHEESE DIP

Preparation Time: 10 minutes
Cooking Time: 1 hour
Servings: 2
Ingredients:
* 1 tsp taco seasoning
* ¾ cup tomatoes with green chilies
* oz. Velveeta cheese, cut into cube

Directions:
1.   Add cheese into the slow cooker. Cover and cook on low for 30 minutes. Stir occasionally.
2.   Add taco seasoning and tomatoes with green chilies and stir well.
3.   Cover again and cook on low for 30 minutes more.
4.   Stir well and serve.

Nutrition:
Calories 159
Fat 12.6 g
Carbohydrates 1.9 g
Sugar 0.3 g
Protein 9.6 g

152.   SALSA BEEF DIP

Preparation Time: 10 minutes
Cooking Time: 1 hour
Servings: 20
Ingredients:
* 32 oz salsa
* lbs. Velveeta cheese, cubed
* lbs. ground beef

Directions:
1.   Brown beef in a pan over medium heat. Drain well and transfer to the slow cooker.
2.   Add cheese and salsa and stir well.
3.   Cover slow cooker with lid and cook on high for 1 hour.
4.   Stir well and serve.

Nutrition:
Calories 279
Fat 17.9 g
Carbohydrates 3.4 g
Sugar 1.6 g
Protein 25.8 g
Cholesterol 88 mg

153.   APPLESAUCE

Preparation Time: 10 minutes
Cooking Time: 2 hours
Servings: 2
Ingredients:
* lbs. fresh apples, peel, core, and slice
* 1/4 cup water
* whole cinnamon sticks
* tbsp. fresh lemon juice

Directions:
1.   Add all ingredients to the slow cooker and stir well.
2.   Cover slow cooker with lid and cook on high for 2 hours.
3.   Discard cinnamon sticks and using potato masher mash until you get desired consistency.

Nutrition:
Calories 59
Fat 0.2 g
Carbohydrates 15.5 g
Sugar 11.7 g
Protein 0.3 g
Cholesterol 0 mg

154. CHOCOLATE FUDGE

Preparation Time: 10 minutes
Cooking Time: 2 hours
Servings: 20
Ingredients:
- ½ cups chocolate chips, sugar-free
- tsp liquid stevia
- 1 tsp vanilla extract
- 1/3 cup unsweetened coconut milk

Directions:
1. Add stevia, vanilla, chocolate chips, and coconut milk into the slow cooker and stir well.
2. Cover slow cooker with lid and cook on low for 2 hours.
3. Open the lid and stir until smooth.
4. Grease casserole dish with butter and spread mixture into the dish.
5. Place dish in the refrigerator for 30 minutes or until fudge firm.
6. Cut fudge into the pieces and serve.

Nutrition:
Calories 81
Fat 4.8 g
Carbohydrates 8.5 g
Sugar 7.3 g
Protein 1.1 g
Cholesterol 3 mg

155. ALMOND CHOCOLATE FUDGE

Preparation Time: 10 minutes
Cooking Time: 6 hours
Servings: 20
Ingredients:
- tbsp. almonds, sliced
- ½ cup unsweetened coconut milk
- 1 tbsp. butter, melted
- tbsp. stevia
- Oz unsweetened chocolate chips

Directions:
1. Grease 8" baking dish with butter and set aside.
2. Add chocolate chips, coconut milk, butter, and stevia into the slow cooker and mix well.
3. Cover slow cooker with lid and cook on low for 2 hours.
4. Add almonds and stir fudge until smooth.
5. Pour fudge mixture into the baking dish and spread well. Place dish in the refrigerator for 6 hours.
6. Cut into squares and serve.

Nutrition:
Calories 15
Fat 1.5 g
Carbohydrates 0.3 g
Sugar 0.2 g
Protein 0.2 g
Cholesterol 1 mg

156. CHOCOLATE AND LIQUOR CREAM

Preparation Time: 10 minutes
Cooking Time: 2 hours
Servings: 2
Ingredients:
- oz. crème fraiche
- oz. dark chocolate, cut into chunks1 teaspoon liquor
- 1 teaspoon sugar

Directions:
1. In your slow cooker ,
2. mix crème fraiche with chocolate, liquor and sugar,
3. stir, cover,
4. cook on Low for 2 hours,
5. divide into bowls and serve cold

Nutrition:
Calories 200,
Fat 12,
Fiber 4,
Carbs 6,
Protein 3

157. DATES AND RICE PUDDING

Preparation Time: 10 minutes
Cooking Time: 3 hours
Servings: 2
Ingredients:
- 1 cup dates, chopped
- ½ cup white rice
- 1 cup almond milk
- tbsp. brown sugar
- 1 tsp. almond extract

Directions:

1. In your slow cooker, mix the rice with the milk and the other ingredients, whisk, put the lid on and cook on Low for 3 hours.

2. Divide the pudding into bowls and serve.

Nutrition:

Calories 152,

Fat 5,

Fiber 2,

Carb 6,

Protein 3

158. BUTTERNUT SQUASH SWEET MIX

Preparation Time: 10 minutes

Cooking Time: 3 hours

Servings: 2

Ingredients:

* pounds butternut squash, steamed, peeled and mashed
* eggs
* 1 cup milk
* ¾ cup maple syrup
* 1 tsp. cinnamon powder
* ½ tsp. ginger powder
* ¼ tsp. cloves, ground
* 1 tsp. cornstarch
* Whipped cream for serving

Directions:

1. In a bowl, mix squash with maple syrup, milk, eggs, cinnamon, cornstarch, ginger, cloves and cloves and stir very well.

2. Pour this into your slow cooker, cover, cook on Low for 2 hours, divide into cups and serve with whipped cream on top.

Nutrition:

Calories 152,

Fat 3,

Fiber 4,

Carbs 16,

Protein 4

159. ALMONDS, WALNUTS AND MANGO BOWLS

Preparation Time: 10 minutes

Cooking Time: 2 hours

Servings: 2

Ingredients:

* 1 cup walnuts, chopped
* tbsp. almonds, chopped
* 1 cup mango, peeled and roughly cubed
* 1 cup heavy cream
* ½ tsp. vanilla extract
* 1 tsp. almond extract
* 1 tbsp. brown sugar

Directions:

1. In your slow cooker, mix the nuts with the mango, cream and the other ingredients, toss, put the lid on and cook on High for 2 hours.

2. Divide the mix into bowls and serve.

Nutrition:

Calories 220,

Fat 4,

Fiber 2,

Carbs 4,

Protein 6

160. TAPIOCA PUDDING

Preparation Time: 10 minutes

Cooking Time: 1 hour

Servings: 2

Ingredients:

* 1 and ¼ cups milk
* 1/3 cup tapioca pearls, rinsed
* ½ cup water
* ½ cup sugar
* Zest of ½ lemon

Directions:

1. In your slow cooker, mix tapioca with milk, sugar, water and lemon zest, stir, cover.

2. Cook on Low for 1 hour, divide into cups and serve warm.

Nutrition:

Calories 200,

Fat 4,

Fiber 2,

Carbs 37,

Protein 3

161. BERRIES SALAD

Preparation Time: 10 minutes

Cooking Time: 1 hour

Servings: 2

Ingredients:

* tbsp. brown sugar
* 1 tbsp. lime juice
* 1 tbsp. lime zest, grated

- 1 cup blueberries
- ½ cup cranberries
- 1 cup blackberries
- 1 cup strawberries
- ½ cup heavy cream

Directions:

1.   In your slow cooker, mix the berries with the sugar and the other ingredients, toss, put the lid on and cook on High for 1 hour.

2.   Divide the mix into bowls and serve.

Nutrition:

Calories 262,

Fat 7,

Fiber 2,

Carbs 5,

Protein 8

162.   FRESH CREAM MIX

Preparation Time: 1 hour

Cooking Time: 1 hour

Servings: 2

Ingredients:

- cups fresh cream
- 1 teaspoon cinnamon powder
- egg yolks
- tablespoons white sugar
- Zest of 1 orange, grated
- A pinch of nutmeg for serving
- tablespoons sugar
- cups water

Directions:

1.   In a bowl, mix cream, cinnamon and orange zest and stir.

2.   In another bowl, mix the egg yolks with white sugar and whisk well.

3.   Add this over the cream, stir, strain and divide into ramekins.

4.   Put ramekins in your slow cooker, add 2 cups water to the slow cooker, cover, cook on Low for 1 hour, leave cream aside to cool down and serve.

Nutrition:

Calories 200,

Fat 4,

Fiber 5,

Carbs 15,

Protein 5

163.   PEARS AND APPLES BOWLS

Preparation Time: 10 minutes

Cooking Time: 2 hours

Servings: 2

Ingredients:

- 1 tsp. vanilla extract
- pears, cored and cut into wedges
- apples, cored and cut into wedges
- 1 tsp. walnuts, chopped
- tbsp. brown sugar
- ½ cup coconut cream

Directions:

1.   In your slow cooker, mix the pears with the apples, nuts and the other ingredients, toss, put the lid on and cook on Low for 2 hours.

2.   Divide the mix into bowls and serve cold.

Nutrition:

Calories 120,

Fat 2,

Fiber 2,

Carbs 4,

Protein 3

164.   PEARS AND WINE SAUCE

Preparation Time: 10 minutes

Cooking Time: 1 hours

Servings: 2

Ingredients:

- green pears
- 1 vanilla pod
- 1 clove
- A pinch of cinnamon
- oz. sugar
- 1 glass red wine

Directions:

1.   In your slow cooker, mix wine with sugar, vanilla and cinnamon.

2.   Add pears and clove, cover slow cooker and cook on High for 1 hour and 30 minutes.

3.   Transfer pears to bowls and serve with the wine sauce all over.

Nutrition:

Calories 162,

Fat 4,

Fiber 3,

Carbs 6,

Protein 3

165. CREAMY RHUBARB AND PLUMS BOWLS

Preparation Time: 10 minutes
Cooking Time: 2 hours
Servings: 2
Ingredients:

- 1 cup plums, pitted and halved
- 1 cup rhubarb, sliced
- 1 cup coconut cream
- ½ tsp. vanilla extract
- ½ cup sugar
- ½ tbsp. lemon juice
- 1 tsp. almond extract

Directions:
1.   In your slow cooker, mix the plums with the rhubarb, and other ingredients, toss, put the lid on and cook on High for 2 hours.
2.   Divide the mix into bowls and serve.
Nutrition:
Calories 162,
Fat 2,
Fiber 2,
Carbs 4,
Protein 5

166. MASCARPONE BERRY PARFAIT

Preparation Time: 5 minutes
Cooking Time: 0 minutes
Servings: 2
Ingredients:

- 1/3 pint raspberries
- 1/3 pint strawberries
- 1/3 pint blueberries
- 8 oz. mascarpone cheese
- 1 cup heavy whipping cream
- ¾ tsp. liquid stevia
- 1 tsp. pure vanilla extract

Directions:
1.   Whip cream, mascarpone, stevia, and vanilla in a bowl until you get stiff, fluffy peaks.
2.   Spoon into serving cups and mix in berries.
Nutrition:
Calories: 159
Protein: 2g
Carbs: 3g

Fat: 17g
Fiber: 0g

167. LEMON-LIME BARS

Preparation Time: 20 minutes + chilling time
Cooking Time: 35 minutes
Servings: 2
Ingredients:
Crust

- ¾ cup almond flour
- ½ cup butter
- ½ cup erythritol-stevia blend
- ¼ cup coconut flour
- ½ teaspoon sea salt

Filling

- 3 eggs
- 2 tbsp. fresh lemon juice
- 2 tbsp. fresh lime juice
- ½ cup erythritol-stevia blend
- ½ tsp. baking powder
- ½ tsp. pure vanilla extract
- ¼ tsp. sea salt

Topping

- Zest from lemon
- Zest from lime

Directions:
1.   You make the crust first - preheat your oven to 325-degrees.
2.   Prepare a glass pan with a coconut-oil based spray.
3.   Mix all the crust ingredients together.
4.   Press into the bottom of the pan and bake for 15 minutes.
5.   Cool.
6.   To make the filling, simply mix everything together.
7.   When the crust is cool, pour overfilling.
8.   Put back in the oven for 15 minutes.
9.   Check to see if the bars look set.
10.   If still liquidy and jiggly, bake for another 5 minutes.
11.   Cool before chilling in the fridge for 25 minutes or so.
12.   For an extra hit of citrus, sprinkle lemon and lime zest on top!
Nutrition:
Calories: 109

Protein: 3g
Carbs: 3g
Fat: 10g
Fiber: 0g

168. MACADAMIA BROWNIES

Preparation Time: 5 minutes + 30 minutes chilling
Cooking Time: 25 minutes
Servings: 2
Ingredients:

- 10 ½ tbsp. melted butter
- 8 tbsp. softened cream cheese
- 6 eggs
- 4 tbsp. unsweetened dark + natural (non-alkalized) cocoa powder
- 4 tbsp. Sukrin Gold
- 3 tsp. pure vanilla extract
- ½ tsp. baking powder
- Generous handful of crushed macadamia nuts
- Pinch of sea salt

Directions:
1. Preheat your oven to 350-degrees.
2. Put ingredients (minus walnuts) in a mixing bowl and blend together.
3. Fold in nuts.
4. Line a baking dish with parchment paper.
5. Pour in batter.
6. Bake for 20-25 minutes, until the brownies are solid and not liquidy at all.
7. Cool 30 minutes before cutting.

Nutrition:
Calories: 178
Protein: 4.5g
Carbs: 3.5g
Fat: 17g
Fiber: 2g

169. SNICKERDOODLES

Preparation Time: 10 minutes
Cooking Time: 10 minutes
Servings: 2
Ingredients:

- 1 ½ cups almond flour
- 6 tbsp. butter
- ½ cup + 2 tablespoons Sukrin Gold
- 1 egg
- 1 tsp. pure vanilla extract

- ¼ tsp. salt
- ¼ tsp. ground cinnamon
- ¼ tsp. ground nutmeg
- 1/8 tsp. ground cloves

Directions:
1. Preheat your oven to 350°F.
2. Line cookie sheets with parchment paper.
3. In a bowl, mix the almond flour, Sukrin, and salt together.
4. Add in butter, vanilla, and egg.
5. Roll dough into 18 balls.
6. In another bowl, mix 2 tablespoons Sukrin with spices.
7. Roll cookies in it to coat.
8. Arrange on the cookie sheets.
9. Bake for 8 minutes, then check. If the sides are starting to brown and the middle looks cooked, they are done. If not, bake another 2 minutes.
10. Cool before serving!

Nutrition:
Calories: 94
Protein: 2g
Carbs: 2g
Fat: 9g
Fiber: 0g

170. RED VELVET COOKIES

Preparation Time: 15 minutes
Cooking Time: 15 minutes
Servings: 2
Ingredients:

- 2 cups almond flour
- 2 tbsp. flax meal
- 1/4 cup coconut flour
- 3 tbsp. unsweetened cacao powder
- 1 beet, raw, peeled and diced
- 2 tbsp. apple cider vinegar
- 1/3 cup ghee
- 1/3-1/2 cup erythritol (or Keto sweetener, to taste)
- 1 egg, whisked
- 1/2 teaspoon baking soda
- 1 tsp. vanilla extract
- Dash of salt

Directions:
1. Set oven to 350°F.

2. Puree the beet then put it into the vinegar and ghee.

3. Mix all the cookie ingredients in a bowl until a soft dough forms.

4. Shape small balls from the dough (use a Tablespoon scoop). Press into a round cookie then put onto a parchment paper-lined baking tray. The cookies will spread, so make sure to leave enough room between the cookies. Makes around 24 small cookies.

5. Bake for 12-15 minutes. Let cool before enjoying

Nutrition:

Calories: 227

Fat: 25 g

Net Carbohydrates: 3 g

Protein: 7 g

171. MINI VANILLA CUSTARDS

Preparation Time: 20 minutes

Cooking Time: 9 minutes

Servings: 2

Ingredients:

- 2 tbsp. water
- 1 cup unsweetened almond milk
- 3 large eggs
- Pinch salt
- 1 cup heavy cream
- ¾ cup powdered erythritol, divided
- 1 tablespoon vanilla extract

Directions:

1. Whisk together ½ cup of the powdered erythritol and water in a saucepan over medium heat until the erythritol melts.

2. Divide the mixture among four small ramekins and set aside to cool.

3. Combine the almond milk and cream in a saucepan and cook over medium heat until it starts to steam, then whisk in the rest of the erythritol and the vanilla extract.

4. Beat the eggs in a mixing bowl.

5. Whisk a few tablespoons of the milk mixture into the eggs, then whisk in the rest in a steady stream.

6. Cover the ramekins with foil and place them in the steamer insert in your Instant Pot.

7. Pour in ½ cup water, then close and lock the lid.

8. Press the Manual button and adjust the timer for 9 minutes.

9. If the timer goes off, let the pressure vent naturally, then press Cancel.

10. When the pot has depressurized, open the lid.

11. Remove the ramekins and let the custards cool for 10 minutes then serve warm.

Nutrition:

Calories: 494 kcal

Protein: 18.16 g

Fat: 40.22 g

Carbohydrates: 28.05 g

172. BERRIES WITH COCONUT CREAM

Preparation Time: 5 minutes

Cooking Time: 15 minutes

Servings: 2

Ingredients:

- 1 cup fat-free cream cheese
- ¼ cup coconut chunks
- ½ tsp. sugar-free coconut extract
- ½ cup mixed berries
- 3 tsp. stevia/xylitol/yacon syrup

Directions:

1. Beat cream cheese until fluffy.

2. Put the coconut chunks and stevia inside a blender and puree.

3. Combine using the cream cheese and set in serving plates.

4. Top with berries.

5. Serve.

Nutrition:

Calories 200

Fat 4.5 g

Carbs 17 g

Protein 23 g

173. LEMON & LIME SORBET

Preparation Time: 5 minutes

Cooking Time: 140 minutes

Servings: 2

Ingredients:

- 1 cup water
- ¾ cup stevia/xylitol/yacon syrup
- 1 cup fresh lemon juice
- 2 scoops whey protein concentrate 1/2 cup lime juice

- 4 whole lemons or oranges cut in half, flesh removed

Directions:

1. Put the lake, stevia, lemon, and lime juice into a blender and puree.
2. Transfer to a container and freeze for about a couple of hours.
3. Remove from the freezer and puree once more using a blender.
4. Transfer to an airtight container and return to freezer.
5. Serve in lemon/orange cups and garnish with fresh mint.

Nutrition:

Calories 150

Fat 0.3 g

Carbs 8.5 g

Protein 25 g

174. KETO VANILLA CHERRY PANNA COTTA

Preparation Time: 10 minutes

Cooking Time: 10 minutes

Servings: 2

Ingredients:

For the vanilla layer:

- 1 cup heavy whipping cream
- 1/2 tsp. vanilla extract
- 1 tbsp. Walnuts; roughly chopped.
- 2 tbsp. whole milk
- 1 tsp. agar powder

For the cherry layer:

- 1 tbsp. Almonds, roughly chopped.
- 2 tsp. cherry extract
- 1 cup heavy whipping cream
- 1 tsp. agar powder

Directions:

1. Set the instant pot then combine all vanilla layer ingredients in the stainless steel insert. Press the *Sauté* button and stir constantly. Bring it to a light simmer and then press *Cancel* button. Transfer to a large bowl and set aside
2. Clean the pot and pat-dry with a kitchen paper.
3. Put all cherry layer ingredients and stir well. Again, bring it to a light simmer, stirring constantly

4. Pour about the 1/2-inch thick vanilla layer in a medium-sized glass. Put the second layer of the cherry mixture. Repeat the process until you have used both mixtures
5. Garnish with fresh mint and refrigerate for at least 1 hour before serving. (optional)

Nutrition:

Calories: 491 kcal

Protein: 6.82 g

Fat: 50.06 g

Carbohydrates: 5.21 g

175. COCONUT FLAN

Preparation Time: 20 minutes

Cooking Time: 9 minutes

Servings: 2

Ingredients:

- 2 tbsp. water
- 1 cup unsweetened coconut milk
- 3 large eggs
- Pinch salt
- 1 cup heavy cream
- ¾ cup powdered erythritol, divided
- 2 tsp. vanilla extract

Directions:

1. Whisk together ½ cup of the powdered erythritol and water in a saucepan over medium heat until it starts to darken. Divide the mixture among six small ramekins and set aside to cool.
2. Combine the coconut milk and cream in a saucepan and cook over medium heat until it starts to steam, whisk in the rest of the erythritol, and the vanilla extract. Beat the eggs in a mixing bowl then pour a few tablespoons of the warmed milk into it while whisking.
3. Put the egg mixture into the milk mixture and whisk smooth, then pour into the ramekins.
4. Cover the ramekins with foil and place them in the steamer insert in your Instant Pot. Pour in ½ cup water, then close and lock the lid.
5. Press the Manual button and adjust the timer for 9 minutes.
6. If the timer goes off, let the pressure vent naturally, then press Cancel.
7. When the pot has depressurized, open the lid.
8. Remove the ramekins and let the flan cool to room temperature then chill until ready to serve.

Nutrition:

Calories: 488 kcal
Protein: 18.16 g
Fat: 40.22 g
Carbohydrates: 27.75 g

176. KETO LEMON STRAWBERRY CHEESECAKE

Preparation Time: 15 minutes
Cooking Time: 0 minutes
Servings: 2
Ingredients:
- 2 pieces large strawberries
- 3 oz. cream cheese (softened)
- 2 tsp. lemon extract
- 1/3 cup Swerve sweetener
- 3/4 cup heavy whipping cream
- zest of 1 lemon

Directions:
1. Prepare two 8-ounce mason jars.
2. In a mixing bowl, put in the whipping cream, sweetener, and cream cheese. Beat them on high setting until the texture becomes creamy and smooth.
3. Put in the lemon extract. Mix thoroughly.
4. Chop one of the strawberries into small pieces. The other strawberry should be sliced into thin heart-shaped slices.
5. Fill each Mason jar half-way with the cream cheese mixture.
6. Make a layer of chopped strawberries on top of the cream cheese mixture in each jar.
7. Fill the rest of each jar with the remaining cream cheese mixture.
8. Top each jar with the heart-shaped strawberry slices. Arrange the slices to form a flower pattern.
9. Sprinkle some lemon zest at the center of each flower.
10. Put in the fridge to chill. Serve.

Nutrition:
Calories: 474
Carbs: 5.7 g
Fats: 48.2 g
Proteins: 4.5 g
Fiber: 0.4 g

177. KETO POUND CAKE (VANILLA FLAVOR)

Preparation Time: 15 minutes
Cooking Time: 50 minutes
Servings: 2
Ingredients:
- 2 cups almond flour
- 1 cup granular erythritol
- 1 cup sour cream
- 1/2 cup butter (sliced into small squares)
- 2 oz. cream cheese
- 2 tsp. baking powder
- 1 tsp. vanilla extract
- 4 pieces large eggs

Directions:
1. Preheat your oven to 350°F.
2. Prepare a 9" Bundt cake pan and butter it generously.
3. In a mixing bowl, put in the baking powder and almond flour. Mix thoroughly.
4. In a microwave-safe mixing bowl, put in the sliced butter and cream cheese.
5. Microwave them for 30 seconds. Stir the mixture to combine well.
6. Put in the sour cream, vanilla extract, and erythritol into the melted cream cheese mixture. Mix well.
7. Pour the cheese mixture into the mixing bowl containing the flour mixture. Mix well the batter.
8. Put in the eggs into the batter. Mix well.
9. Transfer the batter into the prepared Bundt cake pan. Bake the cake for 50 minutes. Do the toothpick test to make sure that the cake is cooked thoroughly.
10. Take out the cake from the oven. Do not remove it immediately from the Bundt pan. It may crumble during the process. Let the cake cool completely in the Bundt pan for 2 hours or more, even overnight.
11. Take out the cake from the Bundt pan. Cut into 12 slices. Serve.

Nutrition:
Calories: 249
Carbs: 23.23 g
Fats: 20.67 g

Proteins: 7.67 g
Fiber: 2 g

178. KETO CACAO BUTTER BLONDIES

Preparation Time: 15 minutes
Cooking Time: 20 minutes
Servings: 20
Ingredients:

- 6 tbsp. cacao butter
- 6 tbsp. erythritol (powdered)
- 2 tbsp. unsalted butter (softened, room temperature)
- 1 tsp. baking powder
- 2 pieces large eggs (room temperature)
- 1/4 cup almond flour
- 2 1/2 tbsp. coconut flour
- 2 tbsp. coconut cream
- 2 tbsp. walnuts (ground)
- 1/2 oz. dark chocolate (chopped)
- 1 tsp. vanilla bean seeds
- 1 tsp. vanilla extract
- 1 pinch stevia extract
- 1 dash salt

Directions:
1. Preheat your oven to 360°F. Prepare a square baking pan (8") and line it with parchment paper.
2. In a microwave-safe mixing bowl, put in the cacao butter. Microwave it for 90 seconds to melt. Stir the melted butter and make sure that there are no more lumps in it. Microwave again to melt the lumps, if needed. Let it cool completely.
3. Once the melted cacao butter is cooled, mix in the unsalted butter and stir.
4. In another mixing bowl, put in the eggs, vanilla bean seeds, vanilla extract, erythritol, and salt. Mix them well for 2 minutes using an electric hand mixer.
5. Put in the coconut cream into the egg mixture. Mix well.
6. Put in the cooled melted cacao butter mixture into the egg mixture. Continue mixing until the consistency gets dense.
7. In another mixing bowl, sift the almond flour, coconut flour, and baking powder. Mix well.
8. Pour the flour mixture into the cream mixture. Mix well.

9. Put in the chopped chocolate and ground walnuts. Mix well.
10. Transfer the batter into the lined baking pan. Spread out the batter evenly on the baking pan.
11. Bake the batter for 20 minutes. Do not over-bake it. Do the toothpick test to know that it is the right time to take the blondies out from the oven.
12. Carefully take out the entire batch of blondies from the pan, including the parchment paper. Put it on the rack to cool down.
13. Once completely cooled, cut into 20 blondie squares. It is recommended to leave the blondies overnight on the counter before serving.
Nutrition:
Calories: 80
Carbs: 1.6 g
Fats: 7.3 g
Proteins: 2.1 g
Fiber: 0.9 g

179. KETO CREAM CHEESE FROSTED CARROT MUG CAKE

Preparation Time: 10 minutes
Cooking Time: 2 minutes
Servings: 2
Ingredients:
Cake:

- 2 tbsp. almond flour
- 1 tbsp. erythritol
- 1 tbsp. psyllium husk
- 1 tbsp. butter (melted)
- 1 piece large egg (beaten lightly)
- 1 tsp. cinnamon
- 1/2 tsp. vanilla extract
- 1/2 tsp. baking powder
- 1/2 piece small carrot (grated finely)
- 1/4 tsp. ginger (ground)
- pinch of salt

Frosting:

- 1 tbsp. whipping cream
- 1/4 cup cream cheese (room temperature)
- 1/2 tsp. vanilla extract
- 1/2 tbsp. erythritol

Directions:
1. In a food processor, put in all the ingredients for the cake. Blend to combine everything.

2. Pour the blended mixture from the food processor into a microwave-safe mug.

3. Microwave it for 90 seconds on high setting.

4. Remove the cake from the mug. Set it aside to cool down.

5. Cut the cake into two layers. Set aside.

6. In a mixing bowl, put in the cream cheese, vanilla extract, and erythritol. Whip them up using an electric hand mixer. Continue whipping until the texture of the mixture becomes soft and creamy.

7. Put in the whipping cream into the cream cheese mixture. Mix thoroughly for 5 minutes.

8. Get the bottom layer of the cake. Scoop a heaping tablespoon of the cream cheese frosting. Spread the frosting on top of the bottom layer of the cake.

9. Get the top layer of the cake. Gently put it on top of the frosted bottom layer of the cake.

10. Spread the rest of the cream cheese frosting on top of the cake and on the sides.

11. You can chill the cake before serving, or you can serve it right away. Cut the cake in half and enjoy.

Nutrition:

Calories: 229

Carbs: 20 g

Fats: 17.3 g

Proteins: 6 g

Fiber: 15.9 g

180. KETO AVOCADO BROWNIES

Preparation Time: 10 minutes

Cooking Time: 30 minutes

Servings: 2

Ingredients:

- 2 pieces large avocadoes (ripe)
- 100 grams Lily's chocolate chips (melted)
- 4 tbsp. cocoa powder
- 3 tbsp. refined coconut oil
- 1/2 tsp. vanilla
- 2 pieces eggs

Dry Ingredients:

- 90 grams almond flour (blanched)
- 1/4 cup erythritol
- 1 tsp. baking powder
- 1 tsp. stevia powder
- 1/4 tsp. baking soda
- 1/4 tsp. salt

Directions:

1. Preheat your oven to 350°F.

2. In a mixing bowl, put in all the ingredients listed under dry ingredients. Whisk to combine well. Set aside.

3. Cut the avocadoes in half. Scoop out the flesh. Weigh the avocadoes. You will need a total of 250 grams of avocadoes for this recipe.

4. Put the avocadoes in a food processor. Process the avocadoes until the texture becomes smooth.

5. Put in the rest of the ingredients into the food processor one at a time. Process for a few seconds after each ingredient is added into the avocado mixture.

6. Put in the flour mixture into the food processor. Process until everything is well combined.

7. Line a baking dish (12" x 8") with parchment paper. Transfer the avocado batter into the baking dish. Spread the batter evenly on the surface of the baking dish.

8. Bake the batter for 30 minutes. Do the toothpick test to know if the brownie is done. The top surface of the brownie should be soft to the touch.

9. Take the brownie out from the oven. Set it aside to cool down. Cut the brownie into 12 square pieces.

Nutrition:

Calories: 155

Carbs: 9.78 g

Fats: 14.05 g

Proteins: 4.02 g

Fiber: 6.98 g

181. CRUNCH BERRY MOUSSE

Preparation Time: 10 minutes

Cooking Time: 0 minutes

Servings: 2

Ingredients:

- 2 cups Heavy whipping cream
- ½ Lemon, zested
- .25 tsp. Vanilla extract
- 2 oz. Chopped pecans
- 3 oz. Fresh raspberries/blueberries/strawberries

Directions:

1. Whip the cream briskly to form soft peaks.

2.   Stir in the vanilla and lemon zest after the peaks are formed.

3.   Fold in the nuts and berries. Stir.

4.   Cover with a layer of plastic wrap.

Nutrition:

Protein: 3 g

Total Fat: 27 g

Net Carbohydrates: 3 g

Calories: 260

182. ZUCCHINI CHOCOLATE CAKE

Preparation Time: 15 minutes

Cooking Time: 30-40 minutes

Servings: 2

Ingredients:

- 3 cups Almond flour
- 1 tsp. Baking soda
- .25 cups Coconut flour
- .5 cup Cacao powder
- 4 Eggs
- 1 tbsp. Apple cider vinegar
- .25 cup Melted cacao butter
- .75 cup Coconut cream
- 3 tsp. Vanilla extract
- 2 cups grated zucchini
- 6 tbsp. Non-GMO birch xylitol, erythritol, or a blend such as Lakanto
- 1 pinch Salt
- Also Needed: 8 by 8 cake pan

Directions:

1.   Warm the oven in advance until it reaches 350° Fahrenheit.

2.   Cover the pan with baking paper or a spritz of coconut oil or ghee.

3.   Combine the dry fixings and toss with the rest of the fixings until thoroughly combined.

4.   Dump the batter into the cake tin.

5.   Bake until it is no longer wobbly in the middle (approx. 30 to 40 min.). Test the cake for doneness with a sharp knife.

6.   Cool completely and serve plain, or any way you like it.

Nutrition:

Protein: 10.1 g

Total Fat: 26.5 g

Net Carbohydrates: 7.4 g

Calories: 306

183. RICOTTA AND BERRIES DESSERT

Preparation Time: 5 minutes

Cooking Time: 5 minutes

Servings: 2

Ingredients:

- 5 ounces whole milk ricotta cheese
- 1 tablespoon heavy cream
- 3 tablespoons powdered erythritol
- 1 oz. raspberries
- 1 oz. blackberries
- ½ ounce blueberries
- 1 tbsp. lemon zest

Directions:

1.   Take a blender and add ricotta, lemon zest, heavy cream, and erythritol. Mix it until you get a smooth mixture.

2.   Divide raspberries, blackberries, and blueberries into two parts.

3.   Prepare 2 glass cups to assemble this dessert.

4.   Add 2-3 tablespoons of ricotta mixture to the bottom of each glass and top it with a layer of blackberries (or other berries if you prefer).

5.   Repeat step 4 with the remaining ricotta mixture, raspberries, and blueberries until glasses are full.

6.   Serve right away or cover with a plastic wrap and refrigerate for up to 8-10 hours.

Nutrition:

Calories: 224 kcal

Protein: 11.73 g

Fat: 15.09 g

Carbohydrates: 11.09 g

184. STRAWBERRY SHAKE

Preparation Time: 5 minutes

Cooking Time: 0 minutes

Servings: 2

Ingredients:

- 1 ½ cups almond milk
- ½ cup coconut milk, unsweetened or heavy whipping cream
- 5 oz. strawberries
- 2 tbsp. sugar- free vanilla syrup
- 2 tbsp. coconut oil
- Whipped cream or coconut cream, (optional)

- 2 tbsp. chia seeds (optional)

Directions:

1. Put all together the ingredients in a blender, and blend until you obtain a smooth mixture.

2. Put into tall glasses and serve topped with whipped cream if using.

Nutrition:

Calories 276 Kcal

Fat: 27.4 g

Protein: 2.5 g

Net carb: 6.4 g

185. KETO MILKSHAKE SMOOTHIE WITH RASPBERRIES

Preparation Time: 11 minutes

Cooking Time: 1 minute

Servings: 1

Ingredients:

- 1 cup unsweetened plain almond milk

- 1 cup crushed ice

- 1/4 cup heavy whipping cream

- 1/4 cup fresh raspberries

- 2 tbsp. sweetener of choice

- 1 tbsp. cream cheese

- 1/2 tsp vanilla extract

- pinch of salt

Directions:

1. Place cheese in a microwave-safe bowl and microwave for a few seconds until soft.

2. Place all the ingredients into a food processor and blend until very smooth.

3. Adjust the sweetener to your taste.

Nutrition:

Calories 150

Fat 15g

Carbohydrates 3.5g

Protein 2g

CHAPTER 9. SMOOTHIES

186. PEANUT KETO SMOOTHIE

Preparation Time: 5 minutes
Cooking Time: 0 minutes
Servings: 1
Equipment: Blender
Ingredients:

- 1/2 cup almond milk (unsweetened)
- 1 tbsp. nut butter (peanut butter, walnut oil) can be substituted for coconut oil
- 1 tbsp. cocoa powder (preferably organic)
- 2 tbsp. roasted peanuts (salted)
- 1/4 medium avocado
- Stevia to taste, mint, and ice of your choice

Directions:
1. Weigh all ingredients. Then add to a blender or food processor.
2. Mix it well.
3. If the smoothie is too thick, you can add a little milk to change the consistency.
4. If the smoothie is too runny, you can add more cocoa powder or peanuts.

Nutrition:
Calories: 216 kcal;
Fat: 17 g;
Protein: 6 g;
Carbs: 8 g

Tip: This should be consumed immediately after preparation, but if you decide to enjoy it later then stir well before drinking as it may come off.

187. KETO BERRY SMOOTHIE

Preparation Time: 5 minutes
Cooking Time: 0 minutes
Servings: 2
Equipment: Blender
Ingredients:

- 1 cup unsweetened coconut milk
- 1 cup berries (blackberries, blueberries, strawberries, raspberries), frozen or fresh of your choice
- 2 scoops of keto protein (replace with coconut or almond flour)
- 2 tbsp. heavy cream
- Stevia to taste, mint, and ice of your choice

Directions:
1. Add all ingredients to a blender.
2. Mix well.
3. If using ice, add this and stir again.
4. Beat until the consistency you want.

Nutrition:
Calories: 114 kcal;
Fat: 7 g;
Protein: 7 g;
Carbs: 5 g

188. AVOCADO SMOOTHIE

Preparation Time: 5 minutes
Cooking Time: 0 minutes
Servings: 2
Equipment: Blender, Knife
Ingredients:

- 1 whole avocado
- 1 oz. chopped mint
- 1 glass of water
- 1 oz. berries
- 2 oz. heavy cream (20%)
- 1 tbsp. of cocoa powder (optional)
- Cinnamon and stevia to taste

Directions:
1. Weigh all food on a measuring scale.
2. Remove the pit and skin from the avocado.
3. Cut the mint into small pieces for your blender.
4. Place remaining ingredients in the blender and blend at high speed for about 30 seconds to the desired consistency.
Nutrition:
Calories: 515 kcal;
Fat: 43 g;
Protein: 8 g;
Net carbs: 20 g

189. MCT PROTEIN SMOOTHIE

Preparation Time: 5 minutes
Cooking Time: 0 minutes
Servings: 1
Equipment: Blender
Ingredients:

- 1 cup almond or coconut milk
- 1 scoop whey protein powder (preferably keto-friendly protein)
- 1 scoop of MCT powder (or 1-2 tsp. of MCT oil)
- ½ tsp. cinnamon
- Cocoa powder and stevia to taste

Directions:
1. Add all ingredients to a high-speed blender and blend until smooth.
2. If you love iced smoothies, add this!
Nutrition:
Calories: 231 kcal;
Fat: 12 g;
Protein: 25 g;
Carbs: 4 g

190. VANILLA SMOOTHIE

Preparation Time: 5 minutes
Cooking Time: 0 minutes
Servings: 2
Ingredients:

- 1 tbsp. organic vanilla extract
- 3–4 drops liquid stevia
- 1 cup heavy cream
- 1 1/3 cups unsweetened almond milk
- ¼ cup ice cubes

Directions:

1. In a high-speed blender, put all the ingredients and pulse until creamy.
2. Pour the smoothie into two glasses and serve immediately.

Nutrition:

Calories: 252;
Net Carbs: 0 g;
Total Fat: 24.5 g;
Saturated Fat: 14 g;
Cholesterol: 82 mg;
Sodium: 143 mg;
Total Carbs: 3.8 g;
Fiber: 0.7 g;
Sugar: 0.9 g;
Protein: 1.9 g

191. TURMERIC SMOOTHIE

Preparation Time: 10 minutes
Cooking Time: 0 minutes
Servings: 2
Ingredients:

- 2 tbsp. chia seeds
- 1 tbsp. ground turmeric
- 1 tsp. ground cinnamon
- 2 tbsp. MCT oil
- 2 tsp. stevia powder
- 1¾ cups unsweetened almond milk
- ¼ cup ice cubes

Directions:

1. In a high-speed blender, put all the ingredients and pulse until creamy.
2. Pour the smoothie into two glasses and serve immediately.

Nutrition:

Calories: 179;
Net Carbs: 3.2 g;
Total Fat: 19.9 g;
Saturated Fat: 14.6 g;
Cholesterol: 0 mg;
Sodium: 159 mg;
Total Carbs: 7.9 g;

Fiber: 4.7 g;
Sugar: 0.1 g;
Protein: 2.7 g

192. COFFEE SMOOTHIE

Preparation Time: 10 minutes
Cooking Time: 0 minutes
Servings: 2
Ingredients:

- 1 cup brewed coffee
- 2 tbsp. MCT oil
- 1 tsp vanilla extract
- 1/8 tsp stevia powder
- 1 cup heavy cream
- 1 cup ice cubes

Directions:

1. In a high-speed blender, put all the ingredients and pulse until creamy.
2. Pour the smoothie into two glasses and serve immediately.

Nutrition:

Calories: 314;
Net Carbs: 1.9 g;
Total Fat: 36.2 g;
Saturated Fat: 27.8 g;
Cholesterol: 82 mg;
Sodium: 29 mg;
Total Carbs: 1.9 g;
Fiber: 0 g;
Sugar: 0.3 g;
Protein: 1.4 g

193. MOCHA SMOOTHIE

Preparation Time: 10 minutes
Cooking Time: 0 minutes
Servings: 2
Ingredients:
- 1 large avocado; peeled, pitted, and chopped roughly
- 3 tbsp. cacao powder
- 2 tsp. instant coffee crystals
- 3 tbsp. granulated erythritol
- 1 tsp. organic vanilla extract
- ½ cup heavy cream
- 1½ cup unsweetened almond milk
- ½ cup ice cubes

Directions:
1. In a high-speed blender, put all the ingredients and pulse until creamy.
2. Pour the smoothie into three glasses and serve immediately.

Nutrition:
Calories: 208;
Net Carbs: 3.1 g;
Total Fat: 19.9 g;
Saturated Fat: 7.4 g;
Cholesterol: 27 mg;
Sodium: 101 mg;
Total Carbs: 8.5 g;
Fiber: 5.4 g;
Sugar: 0.5 g;
Protein: 2.9 g

194. STRAWBERRY SMOOTHIE

Preparation Time: 10 minutes
Cooking Time: 0 minutes
Servings: 2
Ingredients:
- ½ cup fresh strawberries, hulled
- 8–10 fresh basil leaves
- 3–4 drops liquid stevia
- ½ cup plain Greek yogurt
- 1 cup unsweetened almond milk
- ¼ cup ice cubes

Directions:
1. In a high-speed blender, put all the ingredients and pulse until creamy.
2. Pour the smoothie into two glasses and serve immediately.

Nutrition:
Calories: 72;
Net Carbs: 4.8 g;
Total Fat: 2.6 g;
Saturated Fat: 0.7 g;
Cholesterol: 5 mg;
Sodium: 115 mg;
Total Carbs: 6.1 g;
Fiber: 1.3 g;
Sugar: 3.5 g;
Protein: 6.5 g

195. KETO FLU COMBAT SMOOTHIE

Preparation Time: 5 Minutes
Cooking Time: 15 minutes
Servings: 1
Ingredients:
- ½ cup unsweetened nut or seed milk (hemp, almond, coconut, and cashew)
- 1 cup spinach
- ½ medium avocado (about 75 grams), pitted and peeled
- 1 scoop MCT powder (or 1 tablespoon MCT oil)
- ½ tbsp. unsweetened cacao powder
- ¼ tsp. of sea salt
- Dash sweetener (optional)
- ½ cup ice

Directions:

1. In a blender, combine the milk, spinach, avocado, MCT powder, cacao powder, salt, sweetener (if using), and ice and blend until smooth.
Nutrition:
Calories: 249;
Total Fat: 21g;
Protein: 5g;
Total Carbs: 10g;
Fiber: 8g;
Net Carbs: 2g

196. ALMOND SMOOTHIE
Preparation Time: 5 minutes
Cooking Time: 0 minutes
Servings: 1
Equipment: Blender
Ingredients:
- ½ cup unsweetened almond milk
- 3 oz. almond flour
- 2 tbsp. heavy cream
- Stevia to taste
Directions:
1. Weigh and measure all ingredients and place in a blender.
2. Mix for about 30 seconds at high speed until the nuts are crushed.
Nutrition:
Calories: 450 kcal;
Fat: 36 g;
Protein: 23 g;
Carbs: 5 g

197. SPINACH SMOOTHIE
Preparation Time: 5 minutes
Cooking Time: 0 minutes
Servings: 2
Equipment: Blender, Knife
Ingredients:
- 1 cup chopped spinach
- ½ avocado, skinless and pitted
- ¾ cup unsweetened almond milk
- ¼ cup fresh mint leaves
- Stevia to taste, ice if necessary
Directions:
1. Slice the spinach to fill the cup.
2. Cut the avocado into small cubes
3. Combine all ingredients in a blender.

4. Mix on high until very smooth. Add ice if necessary.
Nutrition:
Calories: 225 kcal;
Fat: 18 g;
Protein: 8 g;
Net carbs: 6 g

198. PARSLEY SMOOTHIE
Preparation Time: 5 minutes
Cooking Time: 0 minutes
Servings: 1
Equipment: Blender, Knife, Lemon Juicer
Ingredients:
- 3 oz. fresh parsley
- 1 cup of water
- ½ lemon (juice)
- ¼ oz. ginger root
- Salt to taste (preferably Himalayan pink salt)
Directions:
1. Weigh all ingredients.
2. Chop the parsley and ginger root (this will make the blender work more comfortable).
3. Squeeze out the lemon juice.
4. Add all ingredients to a blender and blend for up to 5 minutes on high speed until smooth.
Nutrition:
Calories: 50 kcal;
Fat: 1 g;
Protein: 3 g;
Net carbs: 7 g

199. GREEN LEMON SMOOTHIE
Preparation Time: 10 minutes
Cooking Time: 0 minutes
Servings: 2
Equipment: Blender, Knife
Ingredients:
- ½ large avocado
- ½ cucumber
- 1 lemon
- ½ cup water
- 1 cup baby spinach leaves
- 1 tbsp. MCT oil
- 2 scoops protein (keto-friendly)
- Stevia to taste, ice if necessary
Directions:

1.	Peel the avocado and remove the pit. Squeeze out the lemon juice. Slice the spinach leaves to fill the cups.
2.	Add all ingredients to a powerful blender and blend until smooth and creamy.
3.	Depending on how thick you want the smoothie, you can add more water or ice and beat again until you reach the desired consistency.
4.	Try it, adjust the flavors if necessary, and stir again.
Nutrition:
Calories: 610 kcal;
Fat: 33 g;
Protein: 60 g;
Net carbs: 14 g

200. GREEN HERBAL DETOX SMOOTHIE

Preparation Time: 10 minutes
Cooking Time: 0 minutes
Servings: 2
Equipment: Blender, Knife, Peeler
Ingredients:

- 1 cup parsley
- 1 cup spinach
- ½ cup basil
- 1 cucumber
- ½ bell pepper (optional)
- 1 lemon
- ½ ounce ginger root
- 1 glass of water
- Turmeric and salt to taste, ice optional

Directions:
1.	Cut lemon, ginger, cucumber (also, pepper if desired) into smaller pieces.
2.	Lemon can be cut with the peel, depending on the power of your blender.
3.	Add all ingredients to a blender bowl.
4.	Beat on high speed for about 45 seconds, then on low speed for 45 seconds.
Nutrition:
Calories: 63 kcal;
Fat: 1 g;
Protein: 3 g;
Net carbs: 10 g

CHAPTER 10. A 28-DAY MEAL PLAN

Days	Breakfast	Lunch	Dinner	Dessert
1	Cheddar and Broccoli Bake	Paprika Chicken	Chicken Broccoli Dinner	Spicy Pecans
2	Basil Mozzarella Eggs	Rotisserie Chicken	Chicken Casserole	Nacho Cheese Dip
3	Wholesome Keto Avo-Burgers	Crockpot Chicken Adobo	Cauliflower Mash	Easy Texas Dip
4	Cheesy Brussels Sprouts and Eggs	Chicken Ginger Curry	Baked Salmon	Cheese Chicken Dip
5	Eggs in Pepper	Thai Chicken Curry	Tuna Patties	Flavorful Mexican Cheese Dip
6	Naan Bread and Butter	Lemongrass and Coconut Chicken Drumsticks	Grilled Mahi with Lemon Butter Sauce	Salsa Beef Dip
7	Breakfast Tuna Salad	Garlic Butter Chicken with Cream Cheese Sauce	Keto Buffalo Drumsticks and Chili Aioli	Chocolate Fudge
8	Low-Carb Muffins with Whey	Cheese and Prawns	Keto Fish Casserole	Almond Chocolate Fudge
9	Spinach Rolls	Salmon Cake	Butter Mayonnaise	Chocolate and Liquor Cream
10	Cheesy Turkey Bake	Coconut Fish Curry	Meatloaf Wrapped in Bacon	Dates and Rice Pudding
11	Creamy Almond and Cheese Mix	Coconut Lime Mussels	Oven Baked Sausage and Vegetables	Almonds, Walnuts and Mango Bowls
12	Homemade Sausage, Egg, and Cheese Sandwich	Clam Chowder	Keto Avocado Quiche	Tapioca Pudding
13	Chicken Sausage Breakfast Casserole	Calamari, Prawn, and Shrimp Pasta Sauce	Keto Buffalo Drumsticks w/ Chili Aioli and Garlic	Fresh Cream Mix
14	Cheddar-Chive Omelet for One	Sesame Prawns	Coleslaw w/ Crunchy Keto Chicken Thighs	Pears and Wine Sauce
15	Fried Codfish with Almonds	Charred Tenderloin with Lemon Chimichurri	Hot Pork and Bell Pepper in Lettuce	Mascarpone Berry Parfait
16	Shrimp Risotto	Herb Pork Chops with Raspberry Sauce	Zingy Lemon Fish	Lemon-Lime Bars

17	Lemony Trout	Pork Burgers with Caramelized Onion Rings	Keto Fish Casserole w/ Mushrooms and French Mustard	Snickerdoodles
18	Buffalo Pizza Chicken	Pork Chops with Cranberry Sauce	Herbed Salmon	Red Velvet Cookies
19	Braised Lamb	Balsamic Grilled Pork Chops	Lemony Salmon	Berries with Coconut Cream
20	Potato Cauliflower Leek Soup	Pork in White Wine	Roasted Mackerel	Lemon & Lime Sorbet
21	Keto Creamy Bacon Dish	Baked Pork Meatballs in Pasta Sauce	Pork Cutlets w/ Spanish onion	Coconut Flan
22	Eggplant Omelet	Grilled Pork Loin Chops with Barbecue Sauce	Rich and Easy Pork Ragout	Keto Lemon Strawberry Cheesecake
23	Keto Cheese Rolls	Pork Pie with Cauliflower	Festive Meatloaf	Keto Cacao Butter Blondies
24	Tuna in Cucumber	Pork Osso Bucco	Crispy Tilapia	Keto Cream Cheese Frosted Carrot Mug Cake
25	Keto Wraps	Fennel Alaskan Cod with Turnips	Cheesy Chicken Sun-Dried Tomato Packets	Keto Avocado Brownies
26	Savory Ham and Cheese Waffles	Sweet & Spicy Mahi-Mahi	Lamb Leg with Sun-dried Tomato Pesto	Crunch Berry Mousse
27	Classic Spanakopita Frittata	Salmon in Spicy Lime Sauce	One-Skillet Green Pasta	Ricotta and Berries Dessert
28	Pumpkin Muffins with Almond Milk	Fish Soul-Satisfying Soup	Proscuitto-Wrapped Haddock	Strawberry Shake

CONCLUSION

This diet is a dietary plan that followers must follow, and this can be quite hard for some to do. The diet restricts carb intake and in turn leads to a state of ketosis. When in this state, the body makes use of its fat stores for energy and does not require calories from carbohydrate intake.

Ketogenic diet has been shown to have many benefits when it comes to fat loss but it is not for everyone. It is important that the person following the diet must be aware of the benefits and possible consequences that come with it. This will help the individual in deciding whether or not he or she should practice this diet or not.

Ketogenic diet was developed in the 1920s by researchers at Johns Hopkins Hospital. It was designed as a treatment for epilepsy, but modern uses have grown to include weight loss, brain endurance, and more. The diet is high in fat and can be very low in carbohydrates. It is also very strict—you need to take in only a specific number of grams of carbs each day. Often, people on the keto diet eat unlimited meats, but not many fruit and vegetables, which can lead to nutrient deficiencies and an unhealthy risk of heart disease (especially if you're older than 50).

When you begin the keto diet, your body switches from using glucose (a type of sugar) as its main source of fuel to using fat instead—specifically from your fat stores. This means that you'll see fairly large changes in fat mass over time. However, the size of these changes depends on how much fat you have to lose and how quickly you stop gaining weight on the diet. The slower your weight loss, the more stable your weight between the beginning and end of the diet—and the less painful it is over time. For most people, eating a standard amount of calories/day will be enough to see results in 7 days or less. However, if you want to lose more weight or maintain your weight after the diet, you'll need to reduce calories even further.

Are there any health benefits?

Many studies have shown that maintaining a low-carbohydrate intake is linked with improved health outcomes. A study around ketogenic diets found that people who followed a high-fat ketogenic diet had fewer cardiovascular events over time than those who followed a regular high-carbohydrate.

In general, individuals that follow a ketogenic diet will eat more fat and less protein and carbs than normal. This may lead to weight loss in some cases (depending on how much weight is lost). However, losing too much weight can be a problem because protein provides essential nutrients such as calcium, magnesium and potassium. So if you're cutting all carbohydrates out of your diet completely, your body will stop getting all the nutrients it needs from food and may begin getting them from supplements such as fish oil or B12, which are very expensive.

Made in the USA
Las Vegas, NV
03 August 2021